A LIFE *through* LETTERS

CHAR,

HERE IS SOMETHING TO READ ON THE BEACH AND PERHAPS INSPIRE YOU TO PUT PEN TO PAPER!

CHEERS,

A LIFE through LETTERS

AN AGING FATHER'S LEGACY

A SON'S REVELATION

THE BIRTH OF A MOVEMENT

ASHLEY DAVIS

LION PRINCE
PUBLISHING

Published 2016

ISBN: 978-0-9981420-0-5
Library of Congress Control Number: 2016915754

Editing and Book design by Stacey Aaronson

Published by:
Lion Prince Publishing

Some names have been changed to protect the privacy of certain individuals.

Printed in the United States of America

CONTENTS

~⌒~

FOREWORD

I deeply admired and loved my brother, and we were always close despite the nine years difference between us, but we became extremely close after his forced retirement. Watching him cope with the many physical limitations thrown his way was difficult, but it was also an inspiration to me. When he asked me to take his roughly typed book and retype it in the format of the letters, it was truly my pleasure. Reading his thoughts on the people who influenced his life was not only a lesson in positive life skills, but it taught me to have greater compassion, as well as to have more appreciation of any act of kindness shown to me.

Bob's greatest desire was to have the book published, so I tried sending it to several publishing companies—and even sent two chapters to *Readers' Digest*—but with no success. I'm sorry he didn't see that dream come true while he was alive, but I know he would be incredibly proud of Ashley for undertaking the gigantic task of creating written context for the letters and having them published. Ashley's enthusiasm for the project and his desire to honor his father has reminded me once again just how much one person's life can impact another.

—Rebecca "Becky" Thomasson
Starkville, Mississippi
October 2016

My brother has always been a dreamer. Of the three boys born to Robert Gray Davis and Harriet Black Davis, Ashley was always the one chasing dreams and rainbows after the end of the storm. So it was no surprise that he was the one of us who had the desire to write a book based on a series of letters penned by our father.

Perhaps it was the fact that our mother was a teacher, or that our father took up the art of letter writing later in life—Ashley certainly caught the bug from one of them. When our father began to write over twenty years ago, not out of necessity but out of passion, the stories we knew as children became immortalized for our own children. And some stories we would not have known had it not been for his writings.

For the three of us, these letters represent a look into the past—a view of our father, a man we wish we had back. His lifework helping others, counseling inmates, paying rent for a single mother, or gathering toys for needy families at Christmas all contributed to the legacy of the man you are about to meet.

Here's hoping you will come to grasp some of the compassion, enjoyment, empathy, and love that our father had. The world surely could use a little more.

—Benji Davis
Punta Cana, Dominican Republic
October 2016

When Ashley asked me about writing this book, I replied, "Anything that honors Dad and that you are passionate about sounds great to me." Both are evident and accomplished here. As your brother, I can honestly say that Dad would be incredibly proud.

It was always meaningful that we had Dad's letters all these years, but to see them brought together in a book takes that meaning to a whole other level. The fact that others will now be able to benefit from Dad's wisdom is a true gift. He was surely a man of great integrity, generosity, and courage—and a wonderful role model for everyone.

Thank you for honoring him in this way.

—Gray Davis
Saluda, South Carolina
November 2016

INTRODUCTION

I have a question for you: When was the last time you wrote a letter? Not a text or a tweet or a direct message with an emoji, but an actual, honest-to-God letter? You know, one you sat down to write with pen and paper, or even composed on your computer, then printed and mailed. A letter into which you put your attention and devotion, one that told someone how much you cared about them. A letter that said thank you, but was more than a thank-you note. A letter that said, "I'm glad you're in my life and here's why!" A letter that expressed you were sorry or that simply conveyed you were thinking of that person.

If you're like most people, it's probably been awhile.

I remember vividly the letters my grandmother sent me as a child. Although some of them merely told of the mundane day-to-day activities in her life, they fostered a connection that couldn't be replicated in a digital form. There was a togetherness created in the act of writing, a bond that was instant as soon as the mailbox opened. You knew that whatever was penned on paper was important. How could it not be, since someone had cared enough to take the time to go through the process of writing a letter?

Sadly, though, the art of letter writing is a dying one.

What began in the seventh or eighth century B.C. as connecting with words chiseled on stone, later graduated to parchment and then the printing press, allowing the art form to flourish. But as technology and our lives have sped up, our attention spans have become shorter. As a result, we now live in a society that no longer seems to appreciate or understand the need to connect on a more personal and intimate level. This higher level equates to an expansion of thought, one that requires more than 140 characters. In short, we all seem to have dimmed as our smartphone screens have gotten brighter.

I have several goals in publishing this book. First and foremost, the book serves as a tribute to my father. He was a minister and an incredible man who, late in life, decided to put his story on paper in the form of letters to the people and things that shaped his life. By the time he wrote these letters, he was not able to put pen to paper; in fact, he was barely able to hold a pen. A series of illnesses and operations left him with only one hand, and that hand had deteriorated due to neuropathy. But refusing to let that stop him, he typed out his series of letters by clutching a pencil in his shriveled hand and using the eraser to peck out one letter at a time on the keyboard. If he could find the motivation and passion to share his thoughts in a meaningful way through such adversity, it's clear that the emotion had to come from the heart.

The letters have served as an extraordinary foundation for my family and me. In their original presentation, they were my father's memoir in letter form. I believe the world deserves to hear that story—the wisdom within is truly priceless.

My second goal is to create context for the reader. As simply publishing the letters as a collection did not seem the best way to present them to the world, I have sought to convey a systematic understanding around each letter of who my father was and his view of the world, and in turn, display how that view shaped my life.

As I read through them, I discovered that the letters contained four fundamental traits that not only guided my father, but that are essential in anyone's life, be it personal or professional. Those traits are Empathy, Altruism, Fellowship, and Devotion. On reflection, I realized that these four elements were the primary tenets by which my father lived. But I also found other notable themes throughout my father's letters, and those are set off in "interludes" in each section. In organizing the book by these themes, it is my hope that you as the reader can better connect, learn, and grow as you experience the letters yourself.

My final goal with this book is to start a movement. I know it might sound grandiose, but if you don't dream big, you might as well not dream at all. The movement I hope to cultivate is one that brings the art of letter writing back to the forefront of society. Imagine if we could all connect once again in the written form. Could it have a huge and lasting impact on how we perceive the world? I contend that it can.

Let's face it: we are all more connected than ever before, yet we are more isolated. We receive updates from society but we share less of ourselves. Technology has taken over our senses and we have forgotten exactly *how* to connect. In fact, the word *connection* in itself has morphed. Connecting used to mean finding a real and absolute way to have a relationship with someone. Now it means, "Is there Internet here?" If the answer is no, we wonder, "How can I tweet a picture of the coffee I'm about to drink?" It may sound crazy, but this is an incredibly common mentality today—yet it's no way to interact with our fellow human beings. We have to find a way to reconnect with ourselves and in turn, with those around us.

Think about this: Is there someone in your life with whom you wish you were still in contact? Is it a childhood friend? A teacher? A loved one? A family member? If you honestly reflect on it, is there someone you need to connect with to say thank you or I'm sorry or I miss you or simply hello? The beauty of recognizing this necessity and taking action is that one letter leads to an open heart, which leads to another letter. If that spirit can be cultivated, it can indeed turn into a movement, resulting in a writing revolution.

This is precisely the transformation I envision coming from my father's collection of letters—and the movement that could ensue. As you are inspired from this book to write your own letters, I urge you to submit them and the stories behind them at www.ALifeThroughLetters.com. This is the venue I've created where people can connect in a meaningful way through the letters that have changed their lives. Yes, it's a digital-based connection, but my hope is that it will be one with a purpose. As you discover common experiences and are enlightened by each other's stories, my wish is that you will be touched by the raw emotion of the human spirit—precipitating health, healing, and joy in the process.

The letters from my father upon which this book is based were conceived in the early 1990s; however, the genesis of this book began in the rural Mississippi Delta of the 1930s. My father, Robert Gray Davis was born May 4, 1934, when cotton was king of the Delta and the birthplace of the Blues was but a mere 20 miles south in Clarksdale. While Clarksdale has gained fame worldwide, small towns like Lula, Friars Point, Gunnison, Rich, and others have remained mostly unknown, but they nevertheless dot the landscape of the Delta as the mighty Mississippi River snakes its way to the Gulf. Like Lula, where my father spent his formative years, the towns were built mainly on agriculture from rich, sandy soil that stretched from the water's edge. But while the cotton may have been rich, the economics of the Delta were not. My father grew up on the heels of the Great Depression in one of the poorest sections of the country.

At the time my father lived in Lula, the neighboring county of Tunica was the poorest county per capita in the United States. Today, it is lined with casinos, strip malls, and golf courses, and while still poor by our country's standards, the landscape is considerably different. The misfortunes and mistakes of rural Mississippi in the 30s have been laid to bear, and rightly so, throughout news and historical accounts over the past 70 years. And while we have and continue to deal with those issues in our country, there was an abundance of good, hardworking people who were born of that society. Yes, racial tensions and separations were evident, yet there were still pockets of well-meaning souls, black and white, who proudly worked hard every day to provide a life for their families. This was the setting in which my father began to formulate the life that would culminate in these letters—letters written as a reflection on the man he had become and the legacy he wished to leave behind.

In the early 1990s, my father was going through some of his hardest times. Throughout his life, he endured a steady deterioration in his health and quality of life. As this gradual decline took full control, he began to reflect on the passing time. While most of us talk about slowing down to reflect on the things for which we should be grateful, he had no choice: life had dictated that he slow down, and he decided to positively channel what energy he had left into recounting the stories and memories that shaped his life.

The original collection of letters was given to us in a three-ring binder before my father passed away. I have carried that binder with me for the past 20-plus years, sometimes reflecting on it, sometimes letting it sit in a box after a move for a few years. My wife, Juhayna, even took the time to replicate the letters in a leather-bound volume for my family. But regardless of their form or location, the letters were always with me. The stories they told and the lessons they taught have had a profound impact on who I am—on the man, husband, and father I have become. They have served as a guidepost as I have navigated my career, love, death, divorce, and my own frailties. They have been cherished inspiration from a man I have adored since my earliest memories.

For years, I considered our family highly fortunate to have this 125-page collection of my father's life. As I have read the letters over the years, they have continued to remind me of the ideals and foundational principles upon which my father led his life, and which formed the basis of the lessons he taught us.

I had the opportunity some years after my father passed away to meet many of his high school friends. As we sat on the banks of Moon Lake, near Lula, they recounted stories of my father as if he were sitting right next to me. These were stories that wiped away the 15 years since his death, and the 65 years since he last saw some of these friends. One gentleman who was particularly close to my father looked at me and said, "Bobby was a minister long before he was a preacher." You see, even in his youth, he was the person others sought out for the guidance and direction they were seeking. His interactions with people led to his career choices—becoming a minister and then a missionary late in life, after he had been a preacher. He truly had gone full circle.

His goal in Lula and in life was to help others, to give back, to make the world a better place. I've come to realize that these letters were not only his legacy to us; they were his final sermon, his memoir, his guidepost on how to live life with grace, compassion, and tolerance.

My father's book, which he originally titled *Letters to the Past*, is transformed here in my attempt to share it with a greater audience. I always knew something would be done with his writing, but until now I had not reached a point in my own life where I felt comfortable sharing my father's story with others. As I began to understand the impact his letters had on me, however, I realized that the scope and influence of the letters were far larger than my brothers, my mother, or me—larger even than my Aunt Becky, who so willingly helped her brother compile and edit them. I saw the letters as being large enough for the world.

My father may have been born into turbulent times with

volatile socioeconomic surroundings, but that made him who he was, and he passed that down to me. I was always a compassionate child, which I believe was fostered from a very early age by my father. His examples forged my path in life, focusing on the core values of Empathy, Altruism, Fellowship, and Devotion, and further through themes such as Uncommon Gratitude, Acceptance, Generosity, and Selflessness. My father instilled these traits in us, both passively through his actions and expressly through his conversations with us in our formative and adult years.

My goal is that we connect, as writer and reader, with my father around these core themes. By doing so, my hope is that you will begin to reflect on those around you who have influenced your life so that in the end, we can all journey through life with a little more understanding, gratitude, and love for not only ourselves, but for our fellow man. And, perhaps, somewhere along the way, you will put pen to paper and write the letter—or letters—that define who you are and the legacy you will leave behind.

$\mathcal{E}$MPATHY

noun | 'em-pə-thē

The action of understanding, being aware of, being sensitive to, and vicariously experiencing the feelings, thoughts, and experience of another of either the past or present without having the feelings, thoughts, and experience fully communicated in an objectively explicit manner.

While there are many definitions of the word empathy, the one above strikes me as all encompassing. To find true empathy for others can at times be a calling higher than even religion. In fact, I recently read that a person does not have to have religion to establish a moral code; they need only have a degree of empathy.

For many, religion can be the vehicle for empathy, but it is not necessary—my father made this clear in his endeavors throughout his life. As a minister, his path was one paved of religious principles; he lived by a code set forth through spiritual and religious teachings. But at my father's core lived an indelible empathetic understanding of his fellow man. This inner sensitivity is what I always believed set my father apart. It is in many respects what I found most spiritual about him, and in turn what I learned most from being his son.

It is true that my father was an amazing preacher. I vividly remember sitting in church as a child and watching my father in the pulpit. I found great pride in the fact that so many people who sat around me were inspired and touched by his words. When I have told people throughout the years that my father was a Southern Baptist minister, their reaction and questions were interesting: Was I allowed to dance? Listen to music? Date girls? The list goes on. Yet I always found this line of questioning strange because my father did not focus on those types of issues. Not being from the hellfire and brimstone crowd, his was a ministry built on the compassion and hope seen in the Good Samaritan, not in the chastising wrath of eternal damnation.

His path out of the pulpit to that of a home missionary was based on a foundation of empathy. Whether he was setting up a food bank for the needy or taking a group of underprivileged kids on a camping trip, he focused on the person first and the empathy his spirit could impart. He was consistently trying to understand, be aware of, be sensitive to, and vicariously experience the feelings of others in order to find the specific action that would make that person whole, and in turn allow them a better life.

"Empathetic people—dreamers and idealists—have this sort of accidental power . . . And when dreamers unite? Well, that's how we start to change the world."

—Unknown

Changing the world, even a small part of the world we touch, is a dream I imagine many humans possess. When people achieve that, in any degree, we are in awe of their success. Mother Teresa, Gandhi, and Albert Einstein are but a few who come to mind. My father taught me that every one of us can change the world—that is the beauty and the power of the human spirit, and that is what is contained in the letters that follow.

Each of the letters you're about to read is rooted in the unwavering trait of empathy, of understanding your fellow man so that you might be able to help make his or her life richer and more fulfilling. But it is not only their lives to which we bring fulfillment, it is to our own as well. I think we can agree that there is no greater reward, no greater joy, than bringing happiness to others. That is what makes humans, well, human.

The act of bringing happiness to others has been proven time and again to have a boomerang effect; that is, the joy you bring to others comes back in various forms when you least expect it. When you live a dream of changing the world, it is actually a dream of helping others, of lifting the lives of the earth's creatures to another level. In short, we change the world so that others might live better.

Have you ever seen the joy of a child who has been given hope for the first time, or sat quietly and wept with the infirm, letting them know someone cares? These are small gestures that in their own way change a part of the world.

My father's writing represents the depths to which he strove to understand and help his fellow man. Sometimes that involved giving or doing; other times it involved sacrifice and adjustments; and still other times it simply meant living in the moment and being present. Doing nothing more than simply showing up can sometimes make the most profound impact on another person. Yet even in those cases, there were still times when my father stopped and wondered: Could I have done more?

The letters that follow contain my father's attempts—and at times his failure—to walk his empathetic path. As you will read, it is shown in the reflections of a young boy who so badly wanted to go to someone in need, but his own insecurities at the time would not allow him to express himself. It is shown in the compassion of a minister who had at last developed the heart, soul, and courage to comfort a fellow man, realizing that his desire to help did not have to result in knowing the answers, or even knowing what to say. Finally, my father found empathy even in inanimate objects, often conveying that it is not necessary to receive empathy yourself, but rather that it can be found if only you take the time to seek it out.

"Empathy is simply listening, holding space, withholding judgment, emotionally connecting, and communicating that incredibly healing message of 'you are not alone.'"
—Unknown

$\mathcal{A}$ LETTER *to the* STONE MAN

As I mentioned, in the 1950s the Mississippi Delta was an area dotted with a number of tiny towns with between 150 to 300 people. Lula was one of these, having about 400 residents, except for Saturday night when most of the folks came to town after a hard week in the cotton fields that surrounded Lula. I remember my father's stories of his childhood adventures there. I even named one of my dogs after the small town.

Lula's claim to fame in at least three states was that it was located about two miles from Moon Lake, which was known for its good fishing. Legend had it that Moon Lake, which got its name from being crescent-shaped like the new moon, had at one time been a part of the great Mississippi River. Supposedly, during the earthquake of the early 1800s, the course of the river was changed and Moon Lake was formed. As wide as the present Mississippi River, which is very near to Moon Lake, the twelve-mile-long lake almost connects with the Mississippi. My father held fond memories of times at the lake during the summer months.

The most famous landmark on Moon Lake was a place known as Uncle Henry's—a restaurant, bar, and dance hall (and there were rumors of other benefits available as well). It was featured in the works of both Tennessee Williams and William Faulkner, and the club was visited by both writers throughout the years. My father and his friends all had explicit instructions from their parents that "they had better never hear of their going to Uncle Henry's." Since they were all obedient children, they never found out firsthand what went on there, but there was one time when they crept close enough to listen.

Several friends had gone out to visit Peggy Perry, a member of their circle. Peggy and her parents had moved from town to the lake area and happened to live in a house that bordered the "forbidden" property. It was Friday night, which was one of the three nights that exciting things could happen at Uncle Henry's, so they decided that since they were so close, they would sneak in the darkness through Peggy's backyard and see what they could discover about Lula's most infamous night spot.

A major part of the building was a huge screened-in side porch, and they hid down in the shadows to watch and listen. It was all quite exciting, and though they witnessed nothing outstanding, they felt a great sense of accomplishment and bravery. (I had the opportunity to visit Moon Lake several years ago and what remains of Uncle Henry's—it has been remodeled and is now a lovely and respectable dinner club.)

It was at Uncle Henry's that my father first became aware of the "Stone Man." There were several small cabins that joined the driveway up to Uncle Henry's, and the Stone Man apparently lived in one of those (though my father only saw him from a distance). My father did not know his name, and he saw him not more than five or six times during one summer he spent at the lake. The man was always in a bed, beneath one of the many trees that also lined the driveway to Uncle Henry's. My father told us that he was often tempted to break the rule and venture onto the property for a closer look and a conversation with him, but he never did. As he grew older and faced his own infirmity, he felt deeply sorry that he never had the courage to do that.

～❧～

Dear Stone Man,

I feel that I must begin this letter with an apology. This concerns my addressing you as "Stone Man." I do not mean it in a disrespectful way, but it is the only name that I ever knew for you. I apologize for not knowing your real name, and more importantly for the fact that I never took the time or had the courage to find out. I was very young that summer that I saw you in the yard at Uncle Henry's and did not know then the things that I now know. I wish I had, for now I would have no trouble crossing the yard to come to your bedside for a visit.

My friends and I used to see you lying in your bed beneath the shade tree at Uncle Henry's. We had learned that your joints were "frozen" from an arthritic condition, and it was as if your joints had turned to stone. You could not move. It had become your destiny to live out your days bedridden and helpless. I knew that you were not totally alone in this world, for someone had to care enough to move you from the small cabin to the shade tree each day.

You have really been on my mind for the past two or three years. One reason for this is that you fall into my "lost opportunities" bag of goodies. I feel deep regret that I did not come to your bedside and visit with you. I do not know what I would have said, nor if I would have been a welcomed intrusion or a nuisance. But I regret that I did not at least make the attempt to contact you and become acquainted.

Another reason you have been on my mind is that I have experienced my own set of health problems that have brought to the surface my own aloneness, and oftentimes feelings of isolation. When these feelings come to me, I think of you, and the difference I might have made for you. It is at that point that I have the deepest regret of only observing you from a distance.

Up until 1987, I had been able to lead a very active life. Then, my kidneys began to fail, and I found it more and more difficult to function in my usual way. In 1989, after four months of dialysis, I found it impossible to continue to work and I retired on disability. For some years, the progressive kidney failure caused a condition known as peripheral neuropathy, which has resulted in a great deal of loss of the use of my hands and lower legs. Though I am not a stone man, for all practical purposes, I find a sense of hopelessness and helplessness in the continued loss of function, especially hand function. How did you manage to endure your loss and survive as you did? I wish I knew the answer to that question for it would bring new meaning to my life.

My constant fear is that I will eventually lose all use of the hands as I have lost all use of the feet. I can walk with the aid of braces but have not discovered a "brace" to make the feeling in my fingers work. I have learned that today is all I have, and I must make the best of it and not spend a great deal of energy worrying about tomorrow. Perhaps that became your solution and your means of survival too.

One valuable lesson I have learned over the past few years is what I term the ministry of presence. You see, I did not come to you because I did not know what to do or what to say. I guess we spend too much energy thinking that we have to have all the answers. I realize now that it probably would not have mattered what I said, but that I came. That is the ministry of presence—just being there. In my days that followed forced retirement, I would have given my life savings if someone had cared enough to just call or come by for a visit. But for the most part, I was forgotten quickly by the many "friends" I thought I had. It was in this context that I became aware of the meaning of the ministry of presence, and though I cannot do anything to make up for my silence to you, I can share my ministry of presence with others with whom I may come into contact for the rest of my life. And each time I have the opportunity, I will take advantage of it and perhaps in some small way, I can make these actions as a memorial to the "stone man" whom I never took the opportunity to know.

A LETTER *to* BROTHER ANDREWS

While living in Lula, my father attended the Lula Baptist Church. Reverend Henning Andrews was the pastor there and was pastor of the Dundee Baptist Church. He was a good preacher, but more importantly, he was an excellent pastor. My father learned a lot from Brother Andrews, and he kept his spirit alive by ministering in a manner that would befit the man who was an early mentor for my father's career in the ministry.

⟨⟩

Dear Brother Andrews,

It has been some time since I have heard from you. I know it has been my turn to write because I believe you contacted me the last time we talked. I do appreciate your letter and the phone calls I have received since being on dialysis and since the transplant.

I have such fond memories of the time when you were pastor to the people at Lula. You were so good to make the many trips to Memphis when I was in Baptist Hospital for those three weeks and the weeks of recuperation that followed. It was through those rough waters that I began to have an understanding of what it meant to be a pastor and was able to use your presence and ministry to me as a pattern years later when I found myself in a position of being a pastor myself.

Harriet and I co-teach a Sunday School class of ladies aged sixty-six and above. This past Sunday the subject of pastors and ministers came up for discussion. I made the observation to them that people rarely remember what the pastor says from the pulpit, but they will always remember what he does or does not do in times of crisis. I believe that to be true. I do not have recollection of what you said in your sermons, but I do remember your visits to the eighteen-year-old whose world had fallen about him as he endured hospitalization and the uncertainty of the future. Because of this, I was able to develop a sensitivity to the need to pay special attention to people who were in crisis. I'm sorry to say that I have observed a number of pastors who do not seem to have that sensitivity. Guess they did not have the excellent example to follow that I did. I feel for them because they have missed a lot of joy and blessing in their silent non-action. I'm even sorrier for the people in crisis who have no pastor to bring comfort and the message of God's hope.

I want to thank you for your visit to Mom and Dad after Van Jr.'s death. I know you had retired and were some distance from them, but you took the time and expense to go see them. Guess even though we retire, the heart of the pastor keeps on beating.

Guess I'd best close. I just wanted you to know how much I appreciate your ministry to me and my family and how grateful I am to you for the wonderful example you provided for me as I responded to God's call to go and preach.

A LETTER to CLAUDE

In 1974 our family moved from Covington, Virginia, to Lowell, North Carolina, where my father became the pastor of the First Baptist Church. After he had been there for about six months, one of the members asked him if he had heard from Claude Murphy. Not only had he not heard from Claude Murphy, but he had not heard of Claude Murphy. He found out from the inquiring church member that Claude was an elderly member of the church, had been on the inactive list for some years, and was ill with terminal cancer. My father went back to the church and looked at the membership roll—there was no Claude Murphy listed. He quickly learned that their church records had been poorly kept and discovered members who had not been placed on the membership roll at all.

The next day, he went for what would be the first of many visits with Claude and his wife. They lived in a two-bedroom duplex, and Claude spent his days and nights in one bedroom, coming out only to use the bathroom. During the day, he sat in darkness with the window covered, as the cancer that was to take his life was on the side of his face and had spread into one eye. As a result, any degree of light to the eye was painful.

His visits with Claude were short, but frequent. Sometimes they would talk, and sometimes they merely sat in silence. Conversation usually depended on how Claude felt and his degree of pain. The cancer had begun on the left side of his face and continued its path toward his eye and downward toward his lower jaw. It was not a pretty sight, and my father naturally wondered how this once strong and stately individual could endure life as it had come to him. But in all his visits with the Murphys, he never once heard Claude complain or question as to why the misfortune had befallen them. They both seemed to endure with quiet strength. Visiting Claude became one of the most rewarding things my father did in his seventeen years as a pastor.

Dear Claude,

I have thought of you so often in the years that have passed since our last visit. I went by your duplex the other day and thought of you, Mrs. Murphy, and the times of visitation that we shared. I hope you were aware of my deep feelings of respect and love that I felt for you.

Our visits together meant a great deal to me. I had such admiration of your strength and stamina enduring what must have been a lonely and frustrating, as well as painful, experience.

I don't think I ever took the opportunity to tell you that my grandfather, my dad's father, died from cancer that was almost identical to yours. I was only thirteen when he died. We lived fifty miles away, so I did not get to visit frequently. When we did go, my dad would take me in to see him. Then I would leave and Dad would stay awhile. Each time I came to visit you, I would take a trip down memory lane and go into my grandfather's room for a few minutes. Somehow, in my ministry with you, I felt that I was ministering to him.

I remember so vividly the day I visited you and in conversation you made the statement, "I wish I did not have to die now. I wish I could get well for a little while." You began to weep. I had the feeling that this was not just a wish to live a little longer but that you had something else in mind. After a few moments, I asked, "What would you do if you could get well?" I will never forget your response. "I would go to church, visit all of my friends and relatives, and tell them how foolish I had been to leave the Lord out of my life. I would tell them not to make the same mistakes that I made. I would tell them that I love Him and I am at peace with Him, and all would be well with me. I'm sorry that I could not see this sooner." As you continued to weep, I found myself weeping with you. How sad that we sometimes learn too late, but how glad I was that you shared those thoughts with me. I knew then that this realization was the source of your great strength. How I did admire you for that, and how happy I felt in the midst of sadness that you had this desire to tell others of your love for Him.

I made you a promise that day, and I have done my best to keep it. I said to you that it did not seem possible for you to get well, and that I would go and tell others what you had said to me. That seemed to be the only way to tell your story—for me to do it for you. That seemed to please you, and the next Sunday, I told your story as an introduction to the solo that I did. The song was "Wasted Years." It has a beautiful message of challenge to live for the Lord, and though the words were not identical to yours, the message was the same.

So many years have passed and now I am experiencing some of the health problems you experienced. No, I do not have cancer, but I have had to quit work and spend a great deal of my time in isolation as you did. As I do this, I spend some time in reflecting on the events and people of the past. You are an important part of that, and I thank God that we had the opportunity to share together. I hope I was able to give as much to you as you were able to give to me. I know that you and Mrs. Murphy are together again, and I find comfort and assurance that you can walk in the fullness of heavenly light with your *now healthy eyes. I look forward to a time when I can come to your "Heavenly Duplex" and we can visit again. Thank you for your acceptance of me as your minister and your friend. I shall treasure your memory until we meet again.*

 A LETTER *to* RAY

Reverend Ray Patterson was a pastor near Seneca, South Carolina, and for a number of years he served as pastor at Richland Baptist Church near Ward, South Carolina. Richland Baptist was the home church for many members of my mother's family and my father became acquainted with him there. My father wrote to him, not because they were close friends, but because he had observed in him those qualities he admired in a pastor. In essence, my father found him to be exemplary in the group of those who responded to God's calling to serve.

Dear Ray,

It was a delightful surprise when you came by my room during my recent stay at Baptist Hospital! Harriet had come back to the room and told me that she had seen you while on the elevator, and that you had come to be with a family in your church who had someone there who was having a bone marrow transplant. I was impressed that you had traveled a distance of four and one half hours to be there for the family. I know that it must have meant a great deal to the family, as well as to the patient. I was also impressed that you took the time to come by my room and spend a few minutes with us. I know that your schedule was pressing and that your mind was occupied with the needs of your church family. Yet, in spite of that, you spent a few moments with us.

There were several things I experienced and felt as I made the decision fourteen years ago to leave the pastoral ministry and begin my work with the Home Mission Board. Two things stand out vividly in my memory. The first was the realization that after eighteen years in the pulpit, I would finally be able to sit with my family in the pew and experience worship. It had been only on rare vacation times that I was able to do that. The other thing was that, at last, I would have a pastor. Most people do not realize that the pastor has no pastor unless he should be fortunate enough to be in an association that has an alert and active director of missions. I was never so fortunate, and I missed having someone to pastor me. Since beginning my work with the association, I have been a member of three churches and am sad to tell you that I am still looking to be pastored!

I hope your church members realize how fortunate they are to have someone in the pulpit who is also a pastor. I have found that just because there is a body behind the pulpit, there is not necessarily a pastor who ministers to the people. I have been hospitalized nine times during the past two years. Four of those times were during dialysis, and five of them were the transplant and following complications. The man behind the pulpit at our church came three times during the nine hospitalizations. Guess in the game of baseball that is a pretty good average, but in the game of pastoring, I feel it to be most inadequate. The last four times were life-threatening: two episodes of possible rejection and two episodes of blood clots in the right leg. All were endured with no pastor. That is why I appreciate so much your making the trip from Seneca to Winston-Salem. It helps restore my confidence in the pastoral role to see someone who takes that part of their calling seriously.

I do not know the experiences of your church member as he waited for the bone marrow transplant, but I do know what I experienced as I began dialysis and waited on the kidney to come. I want to share some of it with you and other pastors who might perchance have an opportunity to read this letter. The average person probably has no idea of the enormous physical and emotional pain that is experienced in such situations. I know I did not until I began to experience it for myself. My kidney failure began many years ago but was always bearable until about four years ago.

Over the years, the kidney failure had caused a "side line" condition called peripheral neuropathy, a disease not in itself, but a by-product of another illness. Many diabetics experience this by-product. In my case, it began to turn into severe neuropathy in 1986. Neuropathy is caused by a deadening of the nerve endings in the extremities, resulting in a loss of muscle function because the nerves no longer stimulate the muscles. I have lost most of the use of my lower legs, feet, and hands. I can walk only with braces and a cane. My thumbs are *about completely void of function. I heard on a TV health program recently that if you lose your thumbs, you immediately lose 60% of the use of your hands.*

The past four or five years have brought a series of giving up and giving in. Before I experienced difficulty in walking, I began having difficulty in driving. I had a Mazda pickup that was a straight drive. On two occasions I found both feet on the clutch and none on the brake where one should be. That was frightening to me. My feet were so numb that I could not tell where they were. So, I gave in and gave up my truck. That may not sound significant to a lot of people, but it began the grief process of loss after loss in my life. Before too long, my hands were so affected that I could not button buttons, zip zippers, or tie ties or shoes. I could not dress myself, hold a toothbrush, or use a comb. With each loss came a flood of grief. I was having to shift from being independent to being dependent. That has been a difficult and frustrating thing for me.

With the worsening of the kidney failure came intensified nausea and weakness. It became more and more difficult to work. It was an effort to get dressed and get to work. By the time I did that, I was so exhausted that the first hour at work was spent on the couch. Finally, the day of dialysis came. The doctor and nurses at the center told me that I would feel so much better when dialysis began. I was encouraged by that. But after about six months, I asked the nurse when I would start to feel better. I could not tell a lot of difference.

Finally, the day came when I could no longer walk without falling all over the place. Getting in and out of the bathtub *was nearly impossible and I could shower only by holding onto the wall. One needs three hands for that! Then, the ultimate loss came. I had been expecting it but still was not emotionally prepared. That loss was having to quit work and apply for disability. In four short years, I had gone from independent to dependent, from active to inactive, from productive to nonproductive, from a working person contributing to society to a "welfare recipient," and from a socially oriented environment to isolation. My days were filled with dialysis, which I was able to do at home four times a day for an hour each time.*

Harriet and Benji went to school, and I was alone. For the first time in my life, I experienced loneliness. I found myself frequently going to the telephone to see if it still worked. No one called or came on an average day. I had been surrounded by people, people who I thought cared, but where were they now? For eleven and a half years, I had been a member of a pastor growth and support group. Only one of them ever called or came, and that was only two or three times.

For years my wife had told me to quit working so hard. "You're going to kill yourself," she often said. "You'll be dead in two weeks and they will have replaced you and forgotten you." Surely not, I thought. Guess she was right and I was wrong. For the most part, the past world has become silent. I do have one friend who works for the Department of Social Services who calls frequently to check on me. She is my only contact with my eleven and a half years of ministry with the Kings Mountain Baptist Association. It would appear that I am a forgotten entity.

I know that I have rattled on and on, but I wanted to give you a glimpse of the emotions I have experienced and the cause of them. There is the isolation, loneliness, fear, anger, insecurity, sense of worthlessness, disappointment in humanity, etc. In all of this, I have held on to my faith in God, and that has been the sustaining factor to get me through the physical, emotional, and spiritual anguish. I must admit a current struggle to a faith in His church and His people. I haven't given up on that yet, but I am closer to it than I have ever been.

Let me close now. I hope these insights into my struggles will be helpful to you as you minister to those in crisis. I feel that whatever the cause of the crisis, the underlying emotions tend to all be the same, only varying in degrees. Let me encourage you to keep up the good work of pastoring that I observed in your visit to Baptist Hospital. I know you are a source of strength and joy to your people.

UNCOMMON GRATITUDE

A LETTER *to a* PILL

My father wrote to many people in his lifetime, and in his attempt at book writing, he also found himself writing to a hospital. Here, however, he wrote to a pill. You might find this strange, but pills became a vital and significant part of his existence. Especially as a transplant patient, pills became his lifeline and kept him from the dreaded word "rejection."

Each day, my father took eight different kinds of prescription medications and an occasional Tylenol. By action, he learned that there were good pills and bad pills, not so much in the chemical content, but in the effect they had on the body. Even so, a good pill can have bad effects if one has allergic reactions to its contents. My father learned this the hard way back in 1963, when he was given nitrofurantoin for a kidney infection. After two weeks on the stuff, he broke out in a horrible rash and had to be hospitalized for several days. The good part was that the kidney infection cleared up. The bad part was the allergic reaction. Ten years later he learned, when he was given a similar antibiotic, that he was allergic to the whole family. Although pills served his life well at various times, they were definitely not for him.

The pill to which he wrote is one that had both the good and the bad for him. He took it daily and enjoyed certain benefits, but it wasn't always that way.

Dear Prednisone,

I know that each morning I get you out of your bottle and swallow fifteen milligrams of you along with four other medications. Sometimes there is a bitter taste if I do not get you and your friends down with quickness. I am told that you are the cause of the bitterness. How does it feel to be told that you are a bitter pill to swallow?

We first met in 1986. On the first Monday in October, I was at work. I sat on the front row of the large conference room of the Kings Mountain Association office having completed my responsibility of presiding over the meeting of the Pastor's Conference. As I sat there, I became keenly aware of a severe itching on my left arm, near the elbow. I tried not to scratch, but to rub, for I had learned that to rub was better than to scratch. The rubbing would lessen the chances of infection from fingernails. I itched for the rest of the day.

That night I noticed a small knot with a black center had formed in the spot where I had itched. By Wednesday the spot had grown into a cone-shaped sore, and the amount of blackness had increased. There was also a hot redness in the sides of the cone, and I was beginning to experience pain and nausea. I went to the family doctor. He looked at it and told me that I had been bitten by a brown recluse spider. He said he was not giving me an antibiotic because it would do no good. He would give me prednisone. That was our first meeting, and I was most impressed with you. When I woke the next morning, I became quickly aware that there was no more pain and that I could move my arm in any direction. The cone was still there with its black center and its redness, but the pain was gone. I had a burst of energy that told me I could conquer the world if I wanted to do so. I thought you were the wonder drug of the ages. Little did I know that my sense of well-being was to be a false illusion of safety and security.

By the next Wednesday, I was in terrible shape. A second cone had appeared about two and a half inches from the original cone, and the original cone had continued to grow. Red streaks were up my arm and had reached to the armpit. There was tenderness under the arm. It hurt! I had called the family doctor on Monday to tell him some of this and he said, "Oh, it's just a spider bite. You have to expect these things with a bite like this. I don't need to see you again. Time will take care of it."

On Wednesday, I left work and drove the twelve miles to Gastonia, North Carolina. I did not know whom I would see, but I knew I needed medical attention. I stopped at one of those "walk-in" clinics. The doctor looked at my arm and told me he would not touch it. He said that I needed to see a surgeon. He called and made arrangements for me to see Dr. Robert Perkins. I drove across town to his office. The wait was short. Dr. Perkins looked at my arm, called his nurse, told her to call my wife at work, and have her come to his office. Then, he called the hospital and admitted me. The hospital personnel were to meet me at the emergency entrance because I should neither drive nor walk. When my wife arrived, he told her that he would do his best to save the arm, but he could not guarantee that it would be saved. He was a "miracle worker," for after ten days I went home with two arms. I am pleased to tell you that I write this with my "spider" arm.

When I was at the walk-in clinic, the doctor asked what medication the family doctor had given me. I told him about you. He responded that I should throw you in the wastebasket because you were not intended to treat a spider bite. So, I took his advice and chucked you. Sorry about that, but it seemed the thing to do at the time.

However, we were to meet again, and our experience would prove to be both helpful and detrimental. In April of 1990, I received a kidney transplant. When the medications were explained to me following the transplant and the three days in intensive care, you were among the listings. I thought, "I know that fella. We have met before and I remember the delightful high he gave me when I had the spider bite. It will be nice to have that feeling I can conquer the world again."

However, you seemed to have lost that quality for I never experienced it again. Could it be that I angered you when I threw you in the wastebasket and you were holding out on me? In the initial stages of our second encounter, the daily doses were ninety milligrams. This amount would continue for almost two weeks and then be reduced to seventy-five milligrams, which I have taken for over a year. We are bound together for eternity, or until this kidney fails and I have to go back on dialysis. I hope that never happens but will have to accept what comes to me.

After ten or eleven days of our second time together, I began to feel some very strange things. It began when I closed my eyes and tried to sleep. There appeared, as if my eyelids were small movie screens, visions of tubing similar to those used in the IV tubes connected to my arm. The tubing was wound in many different directions and moved with rapid pace. At first they were clear in color, then after a few moments, they turned purple in color, then in a few more moments they were bright red. It was a beautiful sight and I was fascinated by all of it. Then, the fascination would end and the fear would set in, for all of a sudden, the red tubing would begin to separate. In the midst of the separation would appear a sinister red eyeball that had the look of evil in it. The tubing became coarse red hair that had the appearance of a beard surrounding the eyeball. It was so scary, and the only relief I could find was to open my eyes and forget sleep attempts for a while. Looking back on it now, I realize that I should have told the nurses or doctor, and perhaps the rest of my experience would not have happened.

Shortly after this, I began to see strange things and my eyes were not even closed this time. I was on the third floor of the hospital, and in looking out my window, I could see the tops of the trees and the building next door. In the trees and in the doorways and windows next door, I began to see small people. They were not children, but rather adults. They seemed to be playing and having the most fun. They would dart in and out of the doorways and the windows, and they were in the trees, sitting on limbs. They would begin to jump from limb to limb with a great deal of daring. I was concerned that they would hurt themselves, but not one of them ever fell or was injured. I thought it strange that I was never able to see their heads, but I knew that they must have heads because they were talking about me and laughing at me. To be able to talk and laugh, one had to have a head and a mouth. At least I had not lost my sense of reasoning, not yet anyway. I would watch them for long periods of time and wish that I could go out and play with them.

The next night, I began to have even more strange experiences. I had been told by one of the doctors that I was to have a kidney biopsy the next day. This struck fear in me because I had undergone a kidney biopsy a few years before *that was the most horrible experience of my life. I promised myself that I would never do that again. Yet, here it was, staring me in the face. That night, a transporter came to my room and told me that he would take me downstairs for my test, so off we went. When we got downstairs, I was put in a large room with high ceilings. I thought this was the time for the kidney biopsy and dreaded the thoughts of what was to happen. There were other people in the room.*

After I had been there for a few moments, I began to float above the rest. They did not seem to pay any attention to this, and I thought that a bit strange. After all, I had never floated before, nor had I seen anyone float. It was a pleasant experience, and I was surprised that I had no fear of falling. I would float up and then begin to come back down. This was great at first, but soon I realized that though I would go down almost to the floor, I would immediately start up again. I began to be filled with fear because I was aware that to get down was impossible. Was I to float forever? Somehow in my confusion, I thought this was the dreaded kidney biopsy. It wasn't at all like the previous one, and I was pleased with that.

After what seemed like hours, I came down and was taken back to my room. In a few minutes, the nurse came into my room. She said, "Mr. Davis, you should have let me know that you couldn't sleep. I would've given you a sleeping pill." I responded, "Oh, I've been downstairs for my test and just got back." She turned and looked at me and said, "You haven't left this room." I knew then that something was wrong. Every time I closed my eyes to sleep, I began to float. I would beg for someone to get me down, but no one would help. Then, things began to change. It all began to reverse itself. It began to happen when I had my eyes open, and the only relief came when I would close my eyes.

On Wednesday, my whole world came apart. I lost all sense of being and reason. It was the day of the kidney biopsy. I waited and waited, but they never came. All of a sudden, I was in a line, waiting to be biopsied. There were four lines abreast. I was at the front of one of them. As the line began to move toward the doctors who were to do biopsies on all of these people, I began to fear, then to panic. I wanted to turn and run away, but I was being pushed into the hole. There seemed to be no escape. As I began to fall, I reached out and grabbed a tree root that was hanging over the side. As I did this, I heard my wife say, "Bob, stop! You're going to hurt yourself!" I told her to leave me alone. The tree root I had grabbed was the IV pole that was behind my bed and I had knocked it over. I continued to fall, and from that point it was one black hole after another. My son Gray was there, and each time I could be drawn to the hole, I would say, "Help me. I'm going to fall!" He would hold me and tell me that he would not let me fall. That was my only salvation for the moment. This sort of thing went on for most of that day and night and began to be less frequent in time. Horrible things continued to happen, but none as horrible as the huge black holes.

By the next Sunday, I was back to normal and on Monday, I was released to come home. I later learned that this was all a reaction to you. You had become a bad pill for me, *but you continued to be a necessary part of my daily routine of medication to prevent rejection of the kidney. Today, you are once again a good pill, and it is time for me to take fifteen milligrams of you along with four of your friends who are good pills. Thanks for your goodness, and I hope that I will never see your bad side again.*

ACCEPTANCE

A LETTER *to* CHURCH FRIENDS

After my father's first year at the seminary, he returned home for a summer job in secular work. While there, he was asked by his home pastor to be the summer pastor of a mission sponsored by his home church. He told us that he agreed with a degree of excitement and two degrees of fear and trembling.

In spite of his "greenness," he took the opportunity at The Green River Mission. He not only took on the task, he survived, learned, and began to realize that no matter what he would learn at the seminary, he would learn the most through experiences in the school of hard knocks. The folks at Green River were most gracious and appreciative of his enthusiasm. They too survived for a while, and hopefully learned from his efforts as he learned from theirs.

My father's next attempt with "full time" service was after graduation with a Master's of Religious Education degree.

He moved twenty-five miles from seminary to begin work at the First Baptist Church of Shelbyville, Kentucky. This too was a learning experience. He had never experienced the presence of a "power structure" in a church. His home church was small and the power lay in the pulpit, or so he thought. Not once in the three years at seminary did anyone tell him that churches have power structures and that one needed to be aware of them. One also needed to know how to work with, and sometimes around, them. My father realized he was in for a great awakening! While the pastor, a loving and gentle man, caught the brunt of this situation, my father caught the secondary brunt because of his support and allegiance to him. He soon realized that his days were numbered, so he left and returned to seminary. God does, indeed, work in mysterious ways, His wonders to perform! He had called my father to preach, he had sidetracked, and He used a most unpleasant situation to tell my father to get back to seminary and finish the task of preparation to pastor.

After a short term as pastor of the Dupont Baptist Church in Dupont, Indiana, and upon graduation from seminary, he became pastor to the people of the First Baptist Church of Ceredo, West Virginia. We spent a delightful and enriching four years there, and now being "a learned scholar," my father could put into practice all the good stuff he had learned at the seminary.

After a while, he came back to the realization that, though formal education was necessary and valuable, the greater education came from experience. We left West Virginia in 1972, a fact for which my mother would often scold my father. After that, my father pastored in Virginia and North Carolina before beginning his work as a home missionary. His letter to church friends could be written to groupings within many of the churches where he served, for in each were those who became special to my parents.

Before my father passed away, he reconnected with friends special to our family in The First Baptist Church of Ceredo, West Virginia. It is to them that he addressed this letter. They became a part of him and held a dear place in his heart through the remainder of his life. He learned many things from them, but the most important were love and acceptance of the newly graduated, inexperienced person they had honored by calling him to be their pastor. For that, he was eternally grateful.

Dear Friends,

What a delight to receive the get well card today! Your thoughts and prayers are greatly appreciated and are a source of strength and encouragement to us. I have always known the importance of prayer support, but it has taken on a new meaning during these past two or three years. When it became necessary for me to begin dialysis in April of 1989, the word was out not only here in North Carolina, but because of my work as a home missionary throughout various parts of the convention. Many responded with prayers on my behalf, and some called and sent cards of prayer and well wishes. It was powerful and has meant a great deal to all of us. And now you have written to let me know of your continued prayers and

*love. How refreshing for us! I firmly believe that it was the
prayer of folks like you who have made it possible for me to
survive the year of dialysis and to receive a new kidney on
April 18, 1990. The kidney continues to work beautifully, and I
know that the prayers of God's people on my behalf have made
that possible. Thank you for continuing to remember us and for
your continued prayer support. I am still waiting for the return
of feeling and use of my legs and hands. I have lost most of the
use of them because of the kidney failure. I am able to walk
with the aid of braces and a cane and am thankful for that. I
am typing by holding a stick inserted through a piece of tubing
and using the "seek and ye shall find" method. I know that you
will find mistakes herein, but excuse that, please. Sometimes,
my stick will not go where it needs to go.*

*Where have all the years gone since I first came to Ceredo
in 1968? It doesn't seem possible, but I guess the calendar does
not deceive us, does it? Our years in Ceredo were good for us,
and we have so many warm and wonderful memories. You
were so kind to take someone fresh out of the seminary and
allow me to become your pastor. I hope that everyone who
graduates from seminary will have a church just like yours in
which to begin. Harriet still scolds me about leaving West
Virginia. As I read and reread your beautiful card, there are so
many wonderful memories associated with most of the names
there, but there are two or three names that ring no bells of
remembrance. I hope this is because they are new folks, and not
an indication that my mental faculties are leaving me in my
aging years!*

As you will remember, we went to Virginia when we left Ceredo. After twenty-five months we came to North Carolina where I was pastor for four years before going to work with The Home Mission Board as director of church and community ministries for The Kings Mountain Baptist Association. After eleven and a half years, it became necessary for me to go on disability. I have missed my work and would love to be able to return, but it looks as if I will not be able to do so.

Harriet has endured all of my health difficulties like a real trooper. It has not been easy on her or the boys, but we have made it thus far and feel confident that we will be able to endure until the end. Our concerns at present are more for her than for me. On June 20 of this year, she went for her annual physical, which included a mammogram. The mammogram showed a "suspicious" nodule in her left breast. We went to Baptist Hospital in Winston-Salem on July 8 to see a surgeon. He removed the lump that day. On July 10, he called to tell us that it was cancer. She went back that next week for removal of the breast. She began chemotherapy on August 5. She has completed two months of treatment and has done well with it thus far. We are hopeful that will continue. She will continue the treatments until January of 1992. Remember to pray for her during these next few months. She continues to try to teach, but some days she isn't able to make it.

Gray finished the University of North Carolina at Charlotte in 1985. In 1987 he married Lisa Anderson of Lewisville, North Carolina. They had met while students at UNCC. I had the honor and privilege of performing their *marriage ceremony. Having baptized all three of the boys, I had begun a new venture. In May of 1989, Kristina Anderson Davis came into this world. She is a doll and a bundle of energy. Among my other titles, I am now Papaw. Several weeks ago we sent her a package. When it arrived, she and Gray called to thank us. As we talked, she said, "Papaw, I threw a fit today." I said, "You did?" She said, "Yeah, and it was a BIG fit too." When Gray got on the phone, he verified that it was, indeed, a BIG fit. She is something else.*

Ashley is a senior at UNCC this year. He was to graduate last year, but he came home the year that I was on dialysis. He returned to college the June after I had the transplant in April. He is majoring in English and minoring in communications. He hopes to enter the field of public relations when he graduates in May of 1992. He was such a help to us while he was here, especially during and after the transplant. I had many trips to make back to Baptist Hospital in the weeks that followed transplant. For about six weeks, I had lost the use of my legs and was confined to bed or to the wheelchair. He will always have my gratitude and appreciation for his efforts during those trying days. He was a real trooper through it all.

You do not know Benji for he came to live with us while we were in Virginia. He will be eighteen next week. He is the tallest of the three boys and he is an excellent swimmer. He has been on the high school swim team for two years and was named outstanding male swimmer last year. He went to the state in three events and was named to the All Conference Team. He has been a source of joy to us in our aging years. I often think that he is the reason that my mind has remained young and alert, even though my body has deteriorated. Our nest will truly be empty when he leaves. He plans to go to community college for two years, then on to UNCC for the last two.

That's about it for us and our history. I did not mean to go on and on, but I felt I wanted to bring you up to date on our happenings since we left in 1972. Even though the years and geography have separated us, we still feel a closeness to you and The First Baptist Church of Ceredo. Harriet has often commented about her feelings for Gray, the first born. I guess you are special for me too, since you were my first church upon graduation.

I had learned many things at the seminary and had much to learn when I went there. However, the greater lessons were yet to be, and you taught me many of those. They did not teach me in the seminary that each church has a "personality," unique and different unto itself. After being there a short time, I began to see your church personality, and thus, could better understand you, your need, and your expectations. As with people, your personality had many facets to it. I found yours to be warm and genuine for the most part. There were those moments that I caught glimpses of unrest and mistrust, but realizing that this came from a short history of unrest with a former pastor, I could understand and accept this not as directed toward me, but reflective of what you had endured. You taught me patience and understanding. Goodness knows, you had to be a patient and understanding people in order to endure me for four years! After all, you were experienced, and I was still learning.

You taught me the skills and importance of loving and caring. I know no one could have been better to us than you were, especially during my time of illness there. During my bout with hypoglycemia and my absence from the pulpit for nearly four months, you were so kind and caring. I remember the feelings of helplessness and hopelessness that we experienced during that time. It seemed that I would never recover. Finally I called the deacons and told them it might be best if I resigned so that the church could get someone who could be a pastor to the people. They would not hear of it. The church stood by me, continuing to pay my full salary and a supply pastor's salary as well. I had never experienced such love and caring. Thank you for that.

You taught me the importance of being out front as the leader of the pack, but not to get too far out front or I would be in danger of losing contact with the group. That was an important lesson. I have observed some pastors, who in their enthusiasm, get so far out front that they lose all communication with the congregation. At that point, chaos usually sets in and often it becomes disastrous.

Thank you for your acceptance of me as your pastor, and for your love and support while I was there the four years. Thank you, also, for your continued remembrance of us after all these years. We covet your prayers for Harriet that chemotherapy will rid her body of any cancer that might be floating around, and for me, that I might regain some use of my legs and hands.

I hope that all is well with you and yours. I would love to be able to "drop in" for a visit, relive good memories, and learn of what life has brought to you. Perhaps some day that will happen. Until then, take care, and remember that our prayers and love are sent your way.

ALTRUISM

noun | ('æltruːˌɪzəm)

the principle or practice of unselfish concern for the welfare of others; the philosophical doctrine that right action is that which produces the greatest benefit to others

*F*or many people, giving is at the core of their happiness, but have you ever thought about what it is that makes giving so rewarding?

Living one's life in an unselfish manner is an endeavor that bears exponential returns; the simple act of giving can produce gifts far greater than any investment. The smile of a child who has just received a wished-for birthday gift, the softness of an elderly woman's eyes as you help her through a door, the relief felt when someone knows you are praying for them ... these may seem like small gestures with seemingly small results. And perhaps if that were the end of it, the gestures would seem fleeting and insignificant. But the true beauty of altruism is that it goes on. What memory will that child hold and desire to pass on? What will that elderly woman do to impart kindness to another? What favor will those remembered in prayer do for someone else? Giving is a form of love that results in the greater good. This greater good is the impact my father sought out his entire life.

"You have not lived today until you have done something for someone who can never repay you."
—John Bunyan

It is with this spirit that I began to learn from my father what life is all about. I realized early on that giving is at the core of a happy life. I also learned that if something is expected from that giving, it is not truly altruistic behavior.

My father created a life of giving. I fondly remember working at Christmastime in the toy store he created for local families in our community. He collected toys, bikes, and necessities from all over the county from individuals and companies. Some of my best holiday memories were of helping struggling single moms shop for their children. As I walked through the aisles helping them select gifts, I could see the pride in their faces knowing that this Christmas would be different, that it would be one their child would remember—the one that would inspire them and remind them that there is good in the world. It would be the Christmas that reassured them that there is indeed a Santa Claus.

Far too often, I have seen people become involved in charities or nonprofits for the wrong reasons. Perhaps it is to position them in a positive light or to gain an advantage in business. But whatever the reason, they are not sincerely engaged in an altruistic endeavor, though they may help someone along the way.

"As you grow older you will discover that you have two hands; one for helping yourself and the other for helping others."
—Audrey Hepburn

The letters that follow are my father's examples of giving for the pure joy of giving, a spirit that was cultivated by his parents. Early in his life, Dad shared this commitment with his sister as they took part in ministry trips to assist those less fortunate. They had hopes to bring a bit of solace to someone else's world, to be present when others might not approach. These trips resulted in meaningful encounters, and also provided some comic relief to the recipients, as you will read.

My father was raised in the Deep South during troubled times, but he was always a warm soul to those from all backgrounds. This openness is probably one of the most important lessons he taught me. I believe his example helped me develop a broad spectrum of friends and a diversity of thought that has served me well in a world that continues to flatten, and whose borders continue to be erased.

Finally, altruism can at times involve sacrifice. This sacrifice is no more evident than in my father's tribute to the Unknown Donor. As my father struggled with the effects of kidney disease, he was blessed with the gift of life in the same moment someone lost theirs. The ultimate sacrifice of organ donation was something that profoundly impacted my family in ways that still give us hope twenty-five years later. We did not know the specifics at the time, but we later learned that the young donor's family decided to use her death to give life to others. As a parent of two young boys, I cannot imagine the emotional struggle it must have taken to make that decision. Dealing with the loss of a child must be one of the most difficult events in life. To have the ability to think of others in that time of such profound grief and sorrow, to give not just of yourself but also of your child, is the ultimate altruistic behavior. It is the type of act that gives one hope that the human spirit is alive and well, even in the darkest of times.

"Each of us is here for a brief sojourn; for what purpose she knows not, though she senses it. But without deeper reflection one knows from daily life that one exists for other people."
—Albert Einstein

A LETTER *to* HELEN

I have heard it said that people are very fortunate to have one or two very close friends in this lifetime. If that is the case, my father considered himself one of the most fortunate people in the world. In each church he pastored, he and my mother were blessed and were able to develop special and lasting friendships. One who meant a great deal to them was Helen.

Shortly after they moved to Kings Mountain, North Carolina, Helen appeared at their door. She lived up the street and around the corner from my parents with her husband, Leonard. She had come to welcome them to the community and to share some vegetables from her garden. Leonard, they learned, was a master gardener, and Helen was a master cook. Aside from these prized attributes, they were wonderful, loving, and caring people. I remember fondly going to see my parents and having Helen stop by to say hello and spend time with my father. She, especially, was a refreshing presence in his darkest days.

Dear Helen,

How does one of inadequate vocabulary find adequate words to let a very special person know how much you have meant to us, and how much we love and appreciate you for your friendship and kindness to us? I really do not know how to answer my own question, but I feel compelled to make the attempt now.

I remember so well the first time you came knocking on our door with garden goodies in hand. What a delightful experience that was for us! We had lived in virtual isolation for nine years in Shelby. It was a rare experience for someone to come knocking at our door. In fact, on those rare occasions, it was usually someone who was looking for someone else. Kings Mountain is refreshingly different. We have been blessed with good neighbors and good friends like you and Leonard. I feel that the move to Kings Mountain in 1987 was our best move ever, and that God planned and sanctioned it. I shudder to think what our existence would be under our current set of circumstances if we were not here.

I cannot begin to tell you what your visits meant to me during the year of dialysis. It seemed you were always aware that I needed a visit and appeared at my door. And the goodies you always brought! You always had my two favorites—fresh-made cornbread and buttermilk. There is no more delicious meal than that. Then there was the fresh salad, cantaloupe cut into bite sizes, tomatoes, okra, peppers, corn, banana pudding, etc. It was like having a supermarket come to my door. The food was great, but the presence was greater and so meaningful to me.

I especially remember the day I was struggling to fix lunch. For most people, it would not have been a struggle, but it is difficult to get things out of the refrigerator when one has limited use of hands and has to rely on a walker to be able to get around. I always felt I needed at least three hands to do that. Wouldn't that be a strange appearance? Well, I finally got the lunch on the plate, and the plate to the table. Then, I remembered the jar of delicious pickled beets you had brought on one of your visits. I guess that next to the cornbread and buttermilk, pickled beets are my third favorite food. So, with walker in hand, I headed for the refrigerator, got the beets out, loosened the top, and immediately dropped the jar.

What a mess I made! Beet juice was everywhere—from the ceiling to the floor, on the cabinet tops, on the cabinet sides, on

the refrigerator, and on me. How would I ever clean it up? I
knew that if I did not get it up soon, we would have a colored
kitchen. I went to the back door to try to get the mop, which was
kept outside. As I reached for the mop, I lost what little balance
I had and fell. Another mess I had made! I realized that I had
been foolish to go for the mop, so I gave up on that idea and
made my way back into the house thinking, "What will I do
now?" Then it came to me, "Call Helen."

So, I called you and told you I needed help, and you were
here in five minutes, cleaned up the beet mess, and stayed with
me for a while. What a comfort you were to me! The whole event
reminded me of my state of helplessness in tending even to the
simple matters of life. I was still struggling in my grief process
over the loss of the use of my legs and hands, and the events of
the day had further convinced me of my inability to function in
life. So, I sat at the table and wept while I watched you work. I
had hoped you would not see that, but you did. You kept saying
to me, "Don't cry. I will clean it up." And you did. How
grateful I am for a friend like you who is here when I need you!

And, then, there was last night. We had just learned that
the lump that was removed from Harriet's breast on Monday
was cancer, and that she would have further surgery next week
to remove the breast. We suspected this would be the report
from the doctor, but we had hoped we were wrong. After
calling some family members, Harriet said, "Call Helen." I
hesitated because I knew you had been out of town with Nancy
and her own current battles with cancer. I knew that if you
were back from taking her to Duke for her chemotherapy, you

would be tired and need your rest. But still, I wanted you to know about our news. So, I called. Again, you were here in five minutes. Thank goodness I had not created a mess for you to clean this time. Your presence was such a comfort to both of us, but especially to Harriet. After you left, she said, "You know, Helen is the best friend I have." I agreed.

Thank you for being our friend and for always being there when we need you. You are a source of joy and delight to all of us in the Davis household.

A LETTER *to a* HOSPITAL

My father was nine years old the first time he was hospitalized, to have his tonsils removed. He did not remember much about the hospital, but did recall promises of vanilla ice cream while recovering at his grandparents' home. His earliest recollection of actual hospitalization was when he was nineteen.

He was preparing to begin his freshman year at The University of Mississippi (Ole Miss) in 1952 when he became ill. He woke up early one morning with a fever, chills, and a painful knot in his neck. Just after sunrise, his mother took him to see Dr. Kirby, who diagnosed him with strep throat. As a result of his illness, he started college a week late.

He remained ill that entire first semester and had scheduled weekly visits with Dr. Bramlett, who also took care of my grandparents. Each week he received the same report: a low-grade kidney infection, increased temperature, and more of the same or different medicine. This continued to be the case through Christmas and into semester finals. It culminated when my father passed out during gym class.

He was taken to the hospital and admitted, and that was the first of twenty-five hospital stays in his lifetime. After being hospitalized eighteen times at Baptist Hospital in Winston-Salem, North Carolina, that hospital had extreme significance in his life. He used to joke that there should have been a plaque somewhere there with his name on it—he felt as if he was part of the hospital family.

When he started his letter-writing project, my father did think it would be strange to write to a hospital. Yet, when he considered significant events and places in his life, this hospital was most definitely on the list—and very near the top. He walked its halls more times than he could count and slept in its beds during numerous admissions. After all that, he felt he knew Baptist Hospital pretty well.

My father likened the hospital to a church: a building of brick and mortar. But a church, he knew, is more than brick and mortar—it is people. It was in this same context that he thought of the hospital, that it was more than brick, mortar, hallways, examining and operating rooms, labs, offices, chapel, cafeteria, elevators, snack bars, waiting rooms, and parking decks. He thought of it as the people who made it run, and it was to those people of North Carolina Baptist Hospital to whom he wrote when he said, "Dear Hospital."

❧

Dear Hospital,

My first admission with you was in 1981. I had been familiar with two of your sisters—one in Memphis, Tennessee, and one in Louisville, Kentucky, so I knew the quality of your family. My doctor was Dr. Harrison in the urology department. He is a fine man and a splendid surgeon. After he had finished with me and I was on the road to recovery, my lab reports showed that the creatinine, which had been 4.2 on a scale, had dropped to 2.7. This was a marked improvement and the beginning of many miraculous reports I would experience. He had said before surgery that we would hope the creatinine measurement would stop at the 4.2 but did not expect it to decrease. For a few years, it seemed that a "cure" had taken place.

Since 1977, I had begun to have numbness in the big toe on my left foot. The numbness soon progressed to my left foot, then the right foot. It then began its slow but progressive move up toward my knees. I came back to you a few times to see a doctor whose name I do not remember and who is now deceased. In 1987, when the numbness began in my left hand, I felt it was time to return to you, even though the now deceased doctor told me several years before that there was nothing that could be done about the numbness.

Upon my return, I was seen by Dr. Peter Donofrio, a super fine human being of superior intelligence and skill. I have seen him on a regular basis since then, and he has taught me a lot about peripheral neuropathy. It is not a disease within itself,

*but the by-product of a disease. He feels that my neuropathy
has come from kidney failure—not so much the severity of it at
that time, but the longevity of it. It has continued to grow
progressively worse and I do not know where it will end. I do
know that he has done all that is known to do, and I am
grateful to him for his care of me.*

*It was Dr. Donofrio who sent me in the direction of Dr.
Patricia Adams in the nephrology department. Having tried all
else and seeing the lab reports that showed continued rise in
creatinine, he felt that the hope for stopping the neuropathy lay
in the beginning of dialysis.*

*Dr. Patricia Adams is one sharp lady. She is super
intelligent and skilled in the area of treatment of kidney failure,
dialysis, and transplantation. Aside from the above adjectives,
there are words like caring, compassionate, concerned,
understanding, listening, and dedication to serving her fellow
man. She has been a source of strength for me these past two to
three years, and I appreciate the fact that she is there to help
you to minister to those with kidney failure who come your way.*

*It was through Dr. Adams' ministry to me that I met Dr.
Kim Hanson and then Dr. Michael Rohr. Both of these fine
physicians have seen me through the beginning of dialysis and
transplantation. They are skilled, intelligent, and
compassionate. Because of their skill and care, I have a
functioning kidney that I hope will be with me for a long time
to come.*

*There are many doctors I have met along the way, but one
in particular who was and always will be very special to me.*

He, too, is a man of great intellect and skill, but he "touched"
me in ways that the others have not. He is Dr. John Burkart,
and he is also a nephrologist.

Two weeks after my transplant, my world fell apart.
Actually, it had begun three days before that Wednesday. I had
begun to see things and people who were not there. There were
people who appeared in my room, usually hiding behind a
chair in the corner and peeping out at me. I kept wondering
who they were and why they did not leave. Then, there were
many of the same people outside my window, sitting in the trees
and windows. They were everywhere, and some of them
appeared not to have heads but were still talking to each other.
I never did figure out how they could do that. Then, on
Wednesday, I lost all sense of being.

It began with the sensation that there were huge black
holes in the floor of my room and I was falling into the holes. If
it was not the holes, my bed would suddenly be up at the ceiling
and I was always sliding out. It was a horrible experience that
lasted for three or four days. I really felt that my mind was gone
and that perhaps it would never return to me. It was a most
frightening and horrifying experience. Thank God, I have
returned to my old, normal self. Some may not see the return as
an improvement, but I surely can tell the difference!

It was in the midst of my insanity that Dr. Burkart
"touched" me in a special way, and I will never forget what he
said to me. Most of those who came into the room acted as if I
were not there. They carried on conversations with Harriet,
asking her things about me as I lay there in my hallucinations

wondering why they did not ask me how I was. Perhaps in my insane condition, I had become invisible! The only exceptions to this were Dr. Adams and Dr. Burkart.

When Dr. Adams came into the room, I seemed to return to "normal" for the moment. She has that kind of soothing effect on me. With Dr. Burkart, I did not return to normal, but in a fleeting moment of sanity, I remember his saying, "Reverend Davis, try not to worry about this. It isn't your fault. It's the medicine causing it." He was the only one in that four-day period of insanity who gave me an encouraging word, and even though my mind was still confused and I was still frightened, I was able to hear his words of encouragement. As best I could, I held onto those words and can still hear him say them to me.

The second time he "touched" me in a special way was a few days later. It was early on the morning of May 7, 1990, the day I was to be dismissed. Finally, after three weeks and a new kidney, I was going home to Kings Mountain. At seven-fifteen that morning, the telephone rang in my room. It was my nephew, Mike, the elder son of my only brother, Van. He was calling to tell me that his dad had died early that morning.

Mississippi seemed so very far away and impossible for me to go. Harriet left the room and in a little while, she returned with Dr. Burkart. He came to me, placed his hand gently on my shoulder, and told me he was sorry to hear of my brother's death. I had never felt such a soothing touch. It and his voice were filled with care, concern, compassion, and a genuineness. It gave me the strength to endure and was the beginning of the grief and healing process for me.

Having experienced all of these things at Baptist Hospital, is it any wonder that I am so enamored with you and that you are such a significant part of my past? But that is not all, for my most recent experience with you was with Dr. George Plonk, a surgeon who last week operated on my wife for breast cancer. He has become the whipped cream on top of the cake for us. We both are so impressed with his skill, and like the others, his sense of caring and concern.

Within your walls are the finest people in North Carolina. In my ten years of going there, I have encountered many of your people from all areas of work. Do you know that I have never met a "grump" while there? From housekeeping to transportation to gift shop to snack shop to cafeteria to lab to office personnel to nurses to doctors—the spectrum of your personnel have shown care, concern, courtesy, and compassion. How do you accomplish that with so many employees?

I suspect that you know the answer to that, but let me share a clue with you that I have recently discovered. On July 8, when we were there for the removal of my wife's breast lump, I lost my billfold. We were able to retrieve it that day because one of your fine employees had found it and returned it to the security office. His name was Ed Johnson, a certified patient transporter. I wrote to Ed to thank him for finding the billfold and for the safe return of all contents. I sent him a check to help express my appreciation for his kindness and honesty. Yesterday, I received a letter from him with the check enclosed. In the letter he wrote, "I appreciate your thoughtfulness, which included a check with your letter as a reward for the return of *your wallet. However, those of us associated with the medical center are here to serve our fellow man and welcome any opportunity to do so. Your happiness and peace of mind are more than adequate reward for me ..."* Isn't that a beautiful attitude, and is it any wonder that I am so impressed with those who work within your walls?

You have instilled a sense of "family" that comes through loud and clear, and for that, I commend you and praise you. I hope the folks of The North Carolina Baptist Convention are aware of your tower of strength in ministry to them and to those from surrounding states who come your way. Thank you for all you have done for me. You have given me life and renewed faith in the goodness of all the folks who serve at North Carolina Baptist Hospital.

$\mathcal{A}$ LETTER *to an* UNKNOWN DONOR

On April 17, 1990, at 6:45 p.m., the telephone in our home rang. That sound forever changed my family. My father was standing in the kitchen, on his way to the back bedroom, which for almost a year had been known as the dialysis room. It was a small room and everything had been moved out and replaced with a table, a recliner, and his dialysis supplies, which were delivered on a monthly basis.

Going to the dialysis room was a routine Dad had followed for the past eleven and a half months, four times a day.

The room was kept as sterile as possible and could not have movement of air when he did his four daily exchanges of dialysis fluid. This meant no air conditioning in the summer or forced-air heat in the winter.

When the phone rang, my father was already about thirty minutes late starting his treatment. He asked me to please answer the phone. He said that if the call was for him, he would call them back when he had finished his dialysis exchange.

He had been told by his doctor in July of 1989 to get a pager and to keep it with him at all times. There were no cell phones in those days, so the pager would be the way of contact when a kidney became available for him. He received the beeper, and it had gone off many times, but always as a false alarm. He had learned to live with that kind of disappointment.

As he headed for the dialysis room, he heard me say, "He can't come to the phone now. He's doing his dialysis. Can I take a message?" Shortly after, I said, "Dad, it's someone from the transplant team at Baptist Hospital." After all those false alarms, we had received a call that a kidney was available, and my father was one of four possible candidates to receive it.

It is difficult to describe the sense of excitement experienced by the four of us in our house at the time. My parents had bags packed for months, so in ten minutes, they were on the way to Baptist Hospital, a two-hour journey. My younger brother Benji and I followed as soon as we made some phone calls and took care of other business.

As soon as my parents arrived at the hospital, the nurse drew blood and they began the five-hour wait to see if my father was the best candidate for the kidney, or if he would return home to wait yet again. At four-thirty on the morning of April 18, 1990, the call came to the room where he was waiting. The kidney was an almost perfect match.

The donor was a young adult male from the Winston-Salem area who had died in a highway accident. All they could tell us about him was that his death was caused by a head injury, so there was no damage to the kidneys. My father desperately wanted to know more about him, but the doctors told him that due to confidentiality, it wasn't possible. Little did he know how things would turn out with respect to the actual identity of the donor and the family.

Dear Friend,

I hope you will understand when I address you as "dear friend." I know we have never had an opportunity to meet and get acquainted, and that I do not even know your name. And yet, I feel very comfortable addressing you in such a manner. You see, I am the recipient of one of the kidneys you left behind, and I feel that you are very much a part of me. I wish I could know the family you left here so that I could express my appreciation for the gift of life you gave me through them. I feel that their loss must be so great to them, and perhaps in some way, I could repay their kindness with kindness and loving support. Did you know that medical ethics forbid my finding out who you were, and anything about your family? I guess there is a reason for that, but if you had been my son, I would find strength and comfort in knowing.

Today I watched Steel Magnolias for the twelfth time. It is a beautiful movie. Did you have the opportunity to see it while you were here? Each time I see it, I laugh and I cry, then I laugh some more. It is the story of many people, one of whom is a young female diabetic patient who has to go on hemodialysis. She later receives a kidney transplant from her mother. The movie does not spend a great deal of time on the matter of dialysis or on the process of transplantation, and I suppose that is just as well. Those two processes are something that one has to endure to understand. I do not know how much knowledge you had of it while you were here, so I would like to share some of that with you. This way, you will be better able to understand my deep sense of appreciation to you for the use of one of your kidneys. By the way, your other kidney went to a fourteen-year-old male. I did not have the opportunity to meet him because he was on a different floor at the hospital than I was. The last I heard, he was doing well.

In April of 1989, it became necessary for me to begin dialysis. I was to be on peritoneal dialysis, which is a bit better than hemodialysis. In order to do this, I was admitted to the North Carolina Baptist Hospital in Winston-Salem for what was considered a "minor" surgical procedure. By this time, I had already had five "minor" procedures and quite frankly was beginning to wonder about the terminology! Finally, the doctor came to tell me about the sixth minor procedure. I told him that I had finally figured out why they kept calling it minor. He looked at me with a puzzled look and asked what I meant. I told him, "It must mean that the surgeon is under the age of eighteen." *That was the only way I could find meaning in the word "minor."*

My dialysis did not begin smoothly. A catheter was inserted into my left side that was to become my "permanent" lifeline until a new kidney could be found. Through this life tube, I would fill my abdomen four times a day and drain it each time. The dialysis fluid would do its work for about four hours, then I would drain it out along with the poisons it had collected. I would then refill myself with a fresh bag of fluid.

In the beginning stages, the process would not work. The doctor said they would have to do more surgery, and this time, the terminology was changed from minor to major—a thought I did not find very appealing! The plans were to replace the non-working tube, remove the scar tissue from two former surgeries, and remove my omentum. I did not know I had one of those! At any rate, it was to result in a "grand opening" of my abdomen. I reluctantly consented to the procedure with great dread because I do not do pain too well, and I knew that the next few days would be most difficult.

The preparation for surgery was done as quickly as possible, and I was on the "rolling cart" with my designer open-air gown and bonnet, being whisked hurriedly to the waiting area for surgery patients. As usual, it was a hurry-up-and-wait process. So, I waited and tried to keep my mind on anything except the impending surgery. After a while, the anesthesiologist came to tell me what he would be doing. As he talked with me, a nurse came and announced that the doctor had called and said that he decided not to do the surgery. I was to be taken back to my room. Surprise! It was a miracle of deliverance for me that began a series of miraculous happenings.

When the doctor came to the room to talk with us, he said he did not feel right about doing the surgery and had rescheduled it for the next day. My response was to tell him that I had decided not to have the surgery; if I had to go on hemodialysis, then I would do it. Later that evening, the dialysis nurse came in and said, "We are going to try this tube one more time and see if we cannot get it to work." So, she hooked my tubing up to the bag of fluid, filled me up, waited thirty minutes, and began the draining process. Guess what? Another miracle happened, for it worked perfectly and in twenty minutes, all the fluid had drained back out! From that point on, I never had a minute's trouble with filling and draining.

There were also other miracles that happened. Not once during the year of dialysis did I have an infection from the tubing or the dialysis procedure. So many patients have a problem with this.

When the call came on April 17 that there was a kidney available, it was my first time to be called. Others have been called several times, only to have to return home in disappointment to wait a little longer. My wife talked with a man while I was in the hospital who was there for the seventh time and was sent home again to wait. That your kidney was a match for my body was another miracle in the series of miracles, and that I was to get a kidney on the first call was a miracle.

The climax to my series of miracles was in the renewed capacity for life that your kidney has given me. We have gotten along beautifully and your kidney began working as soon as the doctor connected it to me. It has worked perfectly for these fifteen months. I have had problems with medications, but none with your new kidney. I'm very grateful for that.

Most of all, I am grateful that you have made it possible for me to live to see some of my goals in life realized. One of my goals for the past few years is to be able to live to see our youngest son finish his education and be established in life. He will be a senior in high school this fall. We have optimism that your kidney will keep me going for the four years of college. Thank you for making it possible to realize this goal. I will be eternally grateful to you for making this goal a possible reality.

Having said all of this, I find that the words are still inadequate to fully and completely express to you my deep sense of appreciation and admiration and love for you for giving me this gift of life. When I went on dialysis, our middle son Ashley called me at the hospital and asked if he could come home. He was in his second year of college. He said he felt he wanted to come so that he could be of help to me. He came, and he was. He returned to the university after the transplant. This year he had to write his family history as a semester project. Here are his words concerning you and your gift of life to me. Though I have tried, I feel he has exceeded my attempts to let you know how deeply we feel concerning you and your gift to me.

It has been a little over a year since the day Dad received the kidney, and things are on the upswing. My father still has some muscular problems, but the doctors say that will clear up. If it doesn't, it will be small potatoes to the fate that faced Dad without the operation.

We do not know from whom the kidney came. All we were told was that the person died in an automobile accident. I have wondered if he realizes the great impact his generosity, and that of his family, has had on our family. I am truly sorry that he had to die in order for Dad to live. Things do, however, seem to happen for a purpose. I hope he knows the feeling I had when I learned my father had the chance at the life he had been desperately clinging to for that long, painful year. I hope he knows the happiness Dad now gets from being able to hold his only grandchild. Most of all, though, I hope the young man realizes that he, in his untimely exit from this life, was part of my family's miracle. I truly hope he knows this as he looks down from his newfound surroundings. I hope he hears this writer's tearfully honest "Thank you."

So, you see, he does have a better way with words than I do. Also, it gives you a family reaction, and not just my reaction. We have all been touched by the generosity of your gift of life, and we have all been moved by the impact of this miracle of new life that I am now enjoying. Thank you again. My love and prayers are with you and your family. Perhaps someday I will have the opportunity to meet them and thank them in person. Until then, my life is a daily reminder of the family who lost a son, and in the process, gave a life.

Post Script [circa 1994]

Several months have passed since I wrote the above. It seems that what I thought was an impossibility has become a reality. We have had the very special privilege to meet the mother of the one whose kidney I am using.

Upon returning from a visit with my doctor in Winston-Salem, there was a message on our answering machine. It was from Lisa Hallaway, who works with Carolina Life Care in Winston-Salem. The message was that the family of the donor was interested in meeting us. It was a dream come true for me! This was late Friday afternoon, and when I tried to return her call, it was too late. We spent a very long weekend waiting for her office to open on Monday.

In April of 1992, I had written an "anonymous" letter to this family and had indicated a desire to meet them so that I could thank them personally. I knew the "rules," but I still had the desire. The rules were that I could write a letter of appreciation, but I could in no way identify myself or my location. The letter could be passed through the doctor to the donor's family, and it was up to them to respond should they wish to do so. During the year that had passed, I wondered if the family had gotten the letter and what their feelings might be. I feel so blessed because the impossible came about and we were to meet the mother of the accident victim.

Arrangements were made, with Lisa's assistance, and on the Saturday after Easter Sunday of 1993, we met at the appointed place. Lisa, Alice (the mother), and Lucy (Alice's longtime friend) were there when we arrived. With me were Harriet, my sons Gray, Ashley, and Benji, Ashley's fiancée Ashlie, and our granddaughter Kristi.

Alice and I had talked some by telephone prior to the meeting, and she had shared some of the details of her daughter's death. Up until this point, we had thought the kidney came from a young male who was killed in a highway accident. However, it was a young lady, sixteen years of age. Her name was Anna. Our meeting was filled with apprehension and excitement by everyone. After three years of wondering and hoping to meet, could I find the right words to express my appreciation for Alice and her family's gift of life to me?

I soon realized that I was to receive more gifts from this caring lady. It was her friendship, and as we talked, I realized that it was almost as if we had known each other for a very long time. The three of them were so kind and gracious to us, and we quickly bonded as new friends. There was another gift that I received that day. Alice brought me a folder with three pictures of Anna on one side and a beautiful poem written by one of Anna's friends and given to Alice the day after Anna's funeral. It is a beautiful and treasured gift. It is presently being framed and will hang in our den on a wall filled with other mementoes that have special significance for me.

Anna was a beautiful young lady, filled with youth and

excitement in life. It is hard to understand how life can be so quickly snuffed out and why those like Anna have been given such a short time here on Earth. I guess God, in His infinite wisdom, has a rhyme and a reason for calling her home at such an early age, but it is difficult to understand. As I have been privileged to meet Alice and thank her for my gift of life, I feel confident that someday I will have the privilege of knocking on the door of Anna's "mansion" and thanking her personally for allowing me a little more time here with my family.

SIBLING BOND

$\mathscr{A}$ LETTER *to* REBECCA

In my father's immediate family, there were four births: three live and one miscarriage. His brother Van (Bo) was born in August, 1932, my father in May, 1934, and his sister Rebecca in November, 1943. All four, including the miscarriage, occurred on a Friday.

The miscarriage occurred when my father was about four or five. The baby was a boy, and my father often wondered what he would have been like if he had lived. As families did not talk of such things in the early stages of pregnancy, the whole event was shrouded in mystery. All my father remembered was that his mom was sick, and that his dad made the nine-mile journey into town to get the doctor to come to the house. The doctor came, stayed a while, then he left. My father's mom seemed okay after that, so he supposed the doctor had performed some sort of miracle.

The only puzzle in afterthought was that this was the same time that his shoebox disappeared. In those days, the family went to Memphis twice a year. The day's outing had two purposes: one was to visit Uncle Curt and Aunt Poca, one of his dad's brothers and his wife (Aunt Poca was part Indian and her given name was Pocahontas); the other was to buy clothes and shoes for the family, which at that time was Grandma, Grandpa, Uncle Bo, and my father. It was never a shopping spree, only the essential two outfits per season and one pair of shoes per person.

A prized possession from the trip for my father was his shoebox. It became his treasure chest where he could keep his cherished items, and it was his and his alone. Reflecting back, my father recounted that the shoebox somehow became more important than the shoes. Needless to say, he was quite distressed when it disappeared. No one in the family seemed to know what had happened to it.

Years later, he came to understand that the "treasure chest" had become the casket for the little brother he never knew. He was buried beneath the althea bush beside the house. After Dad learned what had happened, he felt a sense of pride and accomplishment that his shoebox had been chosen.

His sister Rebecca was born a few years later and became a perpetual source of joy and comfort to him—she seemed to be the factor that made the family circle complete. After the year of dialysis, the multiple hospital stays during that time, a kidney transplant, and the sudden death of their brother Van, he came to realize full well that there was no guarantee of his tomorrows. All he had for certain was the now. (In reality, even healthy people have no assurance of a tomorrow, but he felt that few people seemed to live with that understanding.) My father believed that those of us who have dealt with sickness might have a more realistic grasp on the importance of now. This belief was his motivation for writing his memoir— a way to sum up and evaluate life as he experienced it.

Rebecca, or Aunt Baba as I have always known her, was a key part of my father's life. She was integral to the work my father completed with his original letter-writing project, and he cherished the memories of days gone by and the joys of their relationship while he was still alive.

Dear Rebecca,

I still remember vividly the night that you arrived. I had been so excited because we were told that a baby was coming to our house. I did not know of such maters and could not figure out how you were coming or where you had been or why it took so long for you to get here. Sometime during that night in November, we (Van and I) were sleepily put into the front seat of the car with Dad driving. Mom was in the back seat, and we made our way on the fifty-mile trip to Oxford to get the baby. I thought that was a strange time for you to decide to appear, but my excitement grew in the anticipation of your arrival. Van and I were taken to Grandmother's house and put to bed in one of the upstairs bedrooms. That in itself was exciting for me, for

I was intrigued by a two-story house. I felt as if I were climbing to some mysterious castle.

Dad left us there and took Mom to the hospital. The next morning he came and woke us up. "You have a sister," he said, and I replied, "I want to go and see." Van was still sleeping. Dad woke him, told him of your arrival, and asked if he wanted to go see. He said, "No," and turned over to go back to sleep. I never could understand his lack of enthusiasm; after all, it was I and not he who was being replaced in position in the family. He was the oldest and nothing could change that; I had been the baby for nine years, and I was being replaced and would enter into the middle-child syndrome, a position in which I have felt quite comfortable for all these years. Van did sometimes have a problem with your existence nonetheless.

I remember when you were about eighteen months, and we had gone to Aunt Jennie's for a few days' visit. Van and I were on the porch and Mom brought you out and told Van to watch you. As it turned out, he did not do a very good job of that. You had a stick in your mouth and fell down the steps. The stick tore into the back of your throat and blood was everywhere. I was so scared and so thankful Mom had told Van to watch you and not me. When I saw all the blood and heard the screaming, I was sure that you were not long for this world. Isn't it amazing what children can survive?

The years came and went and before I knew it, I had completed my first year at the seminary and was home for the summer. Remember, that was the summer of our experiences at the Green River Mission. Was that a summer? I was as green as the name of the mission. I have to look back and chuckle at my lack of experience and find deep appreciation for the patience and endurance of the good people of that community. What a team we made, you at the piano and me at the pulpit! At least you knew where the keys were on the piano, but sometimes, I was not sure where the scriptures were, or where the sermon was for that matter.

Remember the night during the revival that we ate with one of the families? I don't remember their names, but I do remember the cold, lumpy mashed potatoes and the iced tea that was like syrup. I also remember a part of the conversation at the table. The head of the house made the statement that we could have a much better church if we had a preacher who could preach with "fire and brimstone." Remember you looked at me and laughed? Guess you thought that was funny. After a few moments of continuing to give his critique of the pulpit, he added that another thing that would help our church services would be to get someone on that piano who really knew how to play it. At that point, I looked at you, and we both chuckled. We had been judged in sincerity by ignorance, and we both seemed to understand that, and it was okay.

Then, there was the afternoon of visitation when you and I visited the family who never attended church. Don't remember their names either but can still see them in my mind's picture. The house was a wreck. The front door was missing, no screens were on the windows, chickens were walking across the kitchen table and standing in the sink eating whatever they could find. The family was made up of little children—I do not remember the number—running half naked through the house, a mother who looked tired and weary, and a large father with a big beard. If I recall correctly, he was half naked, too. His overalls were fastened across his shirtless shoulders, but it was evident that he did not wear underwear. Guess that is the first I knew that people did not wear underwear! Life has a lot of little lessons, doesn't it?

In the midst of all these memories of that visit on a hot July day, I remember the console color TV. As we left, he made the comment that we should come back and eat with them sometime. Isn't God good in that He never allowed that to happen? I could just imagine sitting at my place, and the chickens and I trying to see who could get the food first!

Those were some days, weren't they? I learned a lot, and I remember with such fondness the moments we shared together there. I will always be grateful for your presence with me.

The years have brought a variety of things to each of us, and we have to adapt to many changes. The one thing that has never changed is the feeling of love that I have for you and the feeling of excitement that I have in having you as my sister. Thanks for being there for me all of these years and for the memories we share.

GENEROSITY

$\mathcal{A}$ LETTER *to* AUNT FANNIE

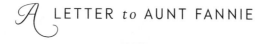

Aunt Fannie was the youngest of my father's in-laws. While she was technically my great aunt, that fact never occurred to me as a child. She was a warm and gentle soul, and I remember many good times we had as children playing on her farm. The central part of the farm was a wonderfully old and inviting home where she lived with Uncle Werner. It always smelled of peach pie, fresh biscuits, and a warm fire.

The original four rooms of the delightful clapboard house were built in the mid- to late-1800s, and three more rooms were added as the family grew. An old rambling house typical of the era, it had a wide open corridor down the middle of the original four rooms that was a wonderful play space.

My mother was the child Aunt Fannie never had, and Mom spent a lot of time as a child and teenager in Aunt Fannie's home. When Aunt Fannie died, and the will was read, my mother had been given the home and twenty-four acres of the land. That little spot in South Carolina remains a cherished part of our family.

Dear Aunt Fannie,

It is a little after three in the afternoon, and if things were as they once were, I know that if I could drive up to your house, I would probably find you, Aunt Tenie, and Aunt Idell sitting on your front porch as you always did in the afternoons, enjoying each other's company and the beautiful scenery surrounding your house. But now I know that I would find none of you there, only a front porch full of memories of the good times that are now past.

In my mind's pictures of your present domain, I suspect that you are sitting on your heavenly porch visiting and looking out upon your most beautiful surroundings. I wonder, do they really have porches in heaven? If they don't, you should speak to the "manager" right away and get one before I get there. I surely would consider it heavenly to be able to join the three of you once again for our afternoon visits.

I would not wish that you could leave your present place of residence to return here, but this world has not been the same since you left us. How we do miss you! Your funeral service was difficult for all of us, but especially for Benji. You were his "grandmother" figure, and it was his first experience of loss by death of someone he loved. How do you explain death to an eight-year-old? You always showed your love to our three boys, and they always knew you loved them and that they were special. Thank you for that. Benji will be a senior in high school this fall and has done well in school. He has also been on the swim team for the past two years. He is the tallest of the three and a joy to both of us in our "aging" years.

There are so many things I would say to you if we could sit on your porch once again and talk. Since we can't, let me attempt to tell you by means of this letter. First and foremost, I want to thank you for your acceptance of me as a bona fide family member. From the very beginning of my entrance into the family by marriage to Harriet, I could sense your acceptance of me. I know that this was due to your love and devotion to Harriet. Others seemed to take much longer for my acceptance, and some seem to still be struggling with this after thirty-one years of marriage. Guess they have yet to realize that for better or for worse, I am here to stay!

I also want to thank you for your kindness to Gray, Ashley, and Benji. How they did like to come to visit Aunt Fannie and Uncle Werner! You showed them, in so many ways, that you loved and cared for them. There were always cokes, candy, and cookies waiting for them and they were always told, "Get what you want." How pleasant it was for them to be able to have access to all of the "goodies" with no restrictions! It wasn't that way in any house in Saluda County except yours. When you left us, a lot of the desire to go to Saluda County went with you.

I want to thank you for all of those times that you were kind and caring to Harriet and me. I remember the times we were in seminary—she worked part-time in the preschool nursery and I raked leaves for one dollar an hour. It kept us going for the most part, but when things got really rough, you seemed to know. Your letters would come just in time to keep the wolf away from the door. There was always some money enclosed, sometimes a little and sometimes a lot, but it was always enough to meet the current need. How did you know what we needed? Perhaps you didn't, but Someone up there with you now must have told you.

And then, there is the matter of the house and the twenty-four acres of land you gave Harriet. What a meaningful gift that was to her! We kept the contents as best we could after the others got their things out of the house. We spent many weekends and vacation days there. We did that for over two years, and then the inevitable happened. Someone broke into the house and took most of the furniture. We went back a few more times, but it was never the same after that.

I did have a most unusual experience there shortly after you left. Somehow, I feel that you are already aware of it, but let me tell you anyway. It was shortly after lunch when I lay down on the bed in the front room. I could see into the kitchen and saw Harriet standing at the sink, tending to the lunch dishes. I lay there thinking how peaceful and serene the surroundings were and how grateful we were to you for giving the house to Harriet. All of a sudden, I heard the screen door open and close on the front porch. I thought, "That's strange," for I had not heard a car drive up or a car door slam. I thought perhaps it was Cora who had walked up to the house to visit as she often did with you.

Then, I heard someone say "Harriet, Harriet." It sounded like your voice. It was eerie to me. I got up off the bed, looked out the front window, saw no one, then went to the front porch. There was no one there and no one in the yard. When I told Harriet about it later, she did not want to stay there. However,

I told her that if it was a visit from you, she would have nothing to worry about because you loved her and would certainly bring her no harm. I have only told a few people this, because the first few I told looked at me strangely and seemed to want to put some distance between us. Wonder why?

I did share it with one person who told me she had heard that when someone dies, their spirit often returns to be sure things are as they wanted them to be, and then, having found the situation to be satisfactory, they go on to their destiny, contented. Her feeling was that you had come for a visit, found satisfaction, and gone on home. It is a lovely thought, and I find some peace in thinking that is what was happening.

Well, I do not know if heavenly beings like yourself get tired of reading my ramblings, but I will stop here and ramble no more. Just wanted to thank you for your love and care for each of us while you were here. You have given us each a wonderful set of memories that we will cherish for as long as we are here on this earth. Be sure to save us a place on your "heavenly porch" so that we can visit each afternoon for all eternity. Benji says to send his love, and that he cannot wait to get on your porch and hear you say, "Get all the coke and cookies you want."

FELLOWSHIP

noun \\'fe-lə-,ship

a friendly relationship among people; the relationship of people who share interests or feelings; a group of people who have similar interests

*T*he above definition of fellowship likely resonates with most people. However, as the world has evolved, fellowship has become much more than just a "friendly relationship" —it now relates strongly to community. Discovering core values and beliefs that others share with you is not only a way of connecting, but it is also a foundational element in finding one's "tribe."

As a child of a minister, I spent many afternoons and evenings in the Fellowship Hall at church—potluck dinners, special speakers, parties, weddings. These events were an important part of my father's focus. In fact, my father built a new Fellowship Hall at the church where he ministered when I was a child. He clearly understood that the church, while based in theology and teaching, was rooted in the foundation of the fellowship between its parishioners, and that he was merely one man giving one message. While it was his duty to convey that message in what he felt was the proper manner, it was the choice of those in attendance to absorb, interpret, and live that message.

⸱ↀↀↀↀↀↀↀↀↀ⸱

Remember and help America remember that the fellowship of human beings is more important than the fellowship of race and class and gender in a democratic society.
—Marian Wright Edelman

⸱ↀↀↀↀↀↀↀↀↀ⸱

Gathering, meeting, and connecting is inherent in what we all seek; each of us is looking for that community with which to associate. Schools, clubs, sports teams, online forums, even coffee shops—they are all based in fellowship.

For me, fellowship is one of the core tenets that has shaped my life. Like many children, I went through a shy phase, but participating with my father in his work provided me with an opportunity to engage in meaningful relationships outside my normal network of friends. It also gave me an understanding that connecting on a human level transcended social and economic barriers.

One of the most important aspects of my father's teaching was that one must have a diversity of experience and thought. I always found great pride in the dichotomy of my father's roots in the American South and his willingness to help all people, without prejudice or judgment. It was this unwavering commitment to equality that I admired and that I continue to work to emulate to this day.

I often accompanied Dad on camping trips he organized

with the local juvenile court system. It was a means of taking troubled kids out of their environment and allowing them to participate in a part of life to which they did not normally have access. It was on these trips that I gained an understanding of being accepted, as I'd spend the weekend with kids with whom I might not have had the chance to associate. These opportunities led me to seek out and relate to people of diverse backgrounds; in fact, I would find myself bouncing from group to group at school, seamlessly interacting and finding fellowship with them all. It never took long to find more similarities than differences, and to help change preconceived notions on all sides.

How many desolate creatures on the earth have learnt the simple dues of fellowship and social comfort in a hospital.
—Elizabeth Barrett Browning

For my father, this need for fellowship became increasingly important as he grew older. His decline in health took a toll not only on his physical being, but also on his emotional and spiritual self. He realized quickly that many of the friends he thought he gained over time were no more than acquaintances. My father had spent so much of his adult life giving back to others that he assumed others would do the same. This reality set in quite firmly once he became homebound. He realized that it was not the *quantity* but rather the *quality* of the connections one builds through life that matter.

The letters that follow are my father's interpretation of

the concept of fellowship—the keeping of a kindred spirit that warms the chill often felt from the realities of life. These bonds are born of various circumstances: they can come in the form of an angel that appears and kindles a fire during the darkest times; in an old friend who makes the effort over the years to stay in touch; in the hospital staff taking extra care of a gentle soul; or in others aging gracefully with gracious hearts, finding fellowship in the journey. As my father reflected on these connections throughout his life, he began to ruminate on the varied ways they shaped him.

The fellowship you share with an individual or group will change over time—along the way, you will likely experience togetherness and happiness, as well as selflessness and possibly regret. When all of these are put together, you will have a shared sense of completeness. That completeness is the essence of fellowship.

Anytime you share life stories with other people, you know, you are acknowledging their humanity and kind of accessing some things about yourself, and other people start to expect things about themselves.
It's kind of like a fellowship.
—Jill Scott

$\mathcal{A}$ LETTER *to* JACKIE HUNT

My father's family moved from Curtis Station to Lula, Mississippi, in the summer of 1950. They had lived in Curtis Station for three years, and my grandparents were employed as principal and teacher at the Curtis Elementary School. They chose this year in particular so that my uncle Van could finish high school in Batesville, as upon investigation of Lula-Rich High School, his parents discovered he would be the only member of the senior class. Talk about a big fish in a little pond! It was doubly worth the wait because Van was valedictorian of his graduating class. (Of course, he would have been valedictorian at Lula-Rich High School should they have made the move in 1949, but it was more impressive to be valedictorian of a class of 180 students than a class of one.)

My uncle may have gotten the brains of the family, but my father claims he got the good looks. When it came time for him to graduate from Lula-Rich High School, he was named salutatorian. No matter that there were only four members of his graduating class! My brothers and I thought this quite funny, and we joked about it often growing up.

Lula had been the childhood home of my grandmother, where she lived into her teenage years. Her mother later moved to Blue Mountain, Mississippi, so that the two daughters could attend Blue Mountain College. After many years, my grandmother returned home. Her father had been the owner of a plantation in the Mississippi Delta, and she inherited a portion of the land. She and my grandfather bought her sister's portion—and if my great-grandfather had not been such an amorous man, my grandmother might have been rich. After five wives and "his," "hers," and "ours" in children, each child received only a small portion of the original plantation. Rumor has it that there were twenty children in all, but no one in the family has been able to verify that. My great-grandmother was the fifth wife, and my father's mother was the last child to be born and survive infancy.

The move to Lula was one of mixed emotions for my father. Fifteen is a difficult time to move, though he guessed it wasn't more difficult than any other age. He did not mind changing schools, but he did hate to leave his friends.

When school started that fall, he was somewhat of a hero, which was a new experience for him. His "heroism" came from the mere fact that he was there—nothing more. You see, there were only ten who had gone out for the football team, and as there were no other male possibilities in the school, the pressure was on for the new kid on the block. He reluctantly became the eleventh member of the group and made it possible for Lula-Rich to have a football team for the next two years. Although he says he was a lousy football player and found no enjoyment in it, he did relish his quick "acceptance" into the student body. (By the way, Dad's team only won one game in two seasons, and that was because the opposing team did not show up, but it was still a "W.")

Despite the emotions involved, the move to Lula brought new friends and held many fond memories for my father. When he reflected on his days at Lula-Rich High School, he thought of friends like Carl Murphree, Bobby Spikes, Lou

Ann Bass, Jackie Haney, Peggy Perry, James Robert Hannah, Ann Pritchard, James Allen Lipsey, Sarah Gillock, and Donna and Jackie Hunt. As I mentioned in the Introduction, I had the chance to meet several of these friends a few years back at the Lula-Rich High School Reunion. I know why they all held special places in his life—they were all kind and caring souls, and they still loved my father immensely, even some 60 years later. But while they all captivated his memory, he chose to write a heartfelt letter to one special friend— Jackie Hunt Foster.

Dear Jackie,

I do not know how many years it has been since I last saw you. It does not seem that long, and yet, it must be at least thirty-five, for I left Lula in 1957 when I went to the seminary in Louisville, Kentucky, and you had left Lula before I did. Haven't the years flown by? I know you will be very much surprised to hear from me after all these years, and perhaps you are wondering, "Why in the world would Bob Davis be writing to me after all of these silent years?"

To clear up the mystery and ease your wondering mind, let me explain. I am in the process of attempting to write a book, and I am entitling it Letters to the Past. It is a book of memories that go back over the years to touch base with significant people and events in my past. You are included in my remembrance of significant people.

Your significance has lasted these forty years since we were together on a night that changed my life, and you had a tremendous impact on my future. By the way, does that word "tremendous" ring any bells? Remember the principal of Lula-Rich who taught our English class? I cannot think of his name, but "tremendous" was one of his favorite and most used words. Several of us had a daily contest to see who could record the most times he said "tremendous." I did not mean to chase that rabbit!

Now, back to your "tremendous" impact on my life. I think it was an August night in 1951, but don't hold me to the exactness of that. In my trips down memory lane, I find that a few of the stepping stones along the way have gotten misplaced. Guess that is part of my aging process. I may not know the exact date, but the events of that night have been permanently planted in my mind.

The youth of Lula Baptist Church went to Memphis to a crusade held at Crump Stadium. That was my first introduction to the "crusade" approach to evangelism, and my first viewing of a stadium. It was quite a contrast to the football field at Lula-Rich High School, wasn't it? Our group sat up near the top and there seemed to be a multitude of people there. The evangelist was a youthful Billy Graham.

I had joined the First Baptist Church at Batesville when I was nine years of age. The main reason for my joining was that my brother, who was eleven, had joined and I wanted to do as he did. I suppose I did have an inkling of what it meant, but the full impact was to come that night in Memphis at Crump Stadium.

*During the progress of the service, I began to feel the
presence of God like I had never felt it before. When the invi-
tation came, I felt a need to respond. There were so many people,
and we were so far up in the stands. I wasn't sure what to do if
I went forward. Could I find the strength to take the first step?
My legs seemed frozen and I was sure that I would fall if I
made the attempt to move them. Billy Graham had been very
explicit in his instructions. "All heads bowed, all eyes closed, no
looking around," he had said. Did I dare break the rules? And
yet I had an overwhelming urge to take a prohibited peek.*

*How thankful I have been all these years that I broke the
"no peeking" rule! When I looked up, there you were in the row
in front of me, making your way to the aisle. Up until that point,
I was sure that if I went, everyone in Crump Stadium would be
looking at me. Then, I thought, "If Jackie can find the courage
to do this, then I can too." So, it was out of your going that I
found the courage to move my frozen legs and take that first
step. It was a step that has meant a great deal to me through
the years, and one that I will never forget, at least as long as I
have my mental faculties. It was a step that has continued to
inspire and encourage me throughout these many years.*

*That night, in addition to the salvation that you helped me
to achieve, I also became aware that God was saying much
more to me. He seemed to be telling me to "go and preach." But
how could that be? Me? Surely I had misunderstood! Yet, the
feeling remained and grew throughout the next few years until I
finally stopped saying no and making all kinds of excuses and
said yes. It was as if I were back in Crump Stadium, and I saw*

you walk in front of me again. I repeated my former thought: "If Jackie can find the courage ..." Then I was able to take another first step. It's been like that all these years. Whenever I faced difficult and seemingly impossible feats, I always went back to my experience at Crump Stadium and the impossible became possible.

In that way I guess, I must be a lot like Jacob was when God's messenger spoke to him after those many years away from home. He told him to go back to Bethel, back to the place he had wrestled with God and found his peace and purpose in life. Crump Stadium was my Bethel, and I have traveled back there in my mind's pictures so very many times. With each visit, I find renewed peace and purpose, and with each visit, I see you making your way down the row in front of me. And, each time I see you, I am grateful for your courage that was an example and inspiration to me then and now.

I hope this letter finds you well, happy, and enjoying the good life.

A LETTER *to* RICHARD WAYNE

Upon entering the Southern Baptist Theological Seminary in Louisville, Kentucky, in the fall of 1957, my father became acquainted with Richard Wayne "Jack" Causey, a fellow Mississippian.

My father never did know why Richard Wayne was known as Jack—one would think that two "first" names were enough.

But he supposed that he didn't like either; he found many people who did not like their names. My Uncle Van was one of those. This was understandable, my father said, since his first name was Lavanda. Dad spent fifty-seven years thanking the good Lord that his brother was the first child and not he. At any rate, he refers here to Richard Wayne as "Jack."

Though Dad and Jack had been seniors together at Mississippi College, they did not meet until their seminary days. After he and Jack became friends, they shared an apartment off campus with two other students, and they were roommates when they returned for their second year. They remained roommates until Jack married Mary Elizabeth that next summer. Dad was in their wedding and Jack was in mom and dad's. Jack became a pastor in Statesville, North Carolina, in the 1980s, and he and my father saw each other and talked by phone on occasion.

Dear Jack,

How nice to receive your phone call the other night! With each trip we make to Baptist Hospital, I think that I will stop in Statesville and call you, but do not do so. It is usually either very early in the a.m., or we are so tired after the hospital ordeal that we want to get on home. Thanks for thinking of us and for the call.

I have appreciated your friendship through the years and have found it to be of special significance in these latter days, as we both have become aware that life is changing for us. My struggles with kidney failure, dialysis, and transplantation, and Harriet's present struggle with cancer have made us keenly aware that today is the reality of what we have, and friends are our greatest acquisition of life. I am pleased to count you and Mary Elizabeth among the friends we have made through the years. I know that each time we talk, we say that the four of us must get together. We must, you know.

Didn't we have some times during seminary days? That first year was very difficult for me, and I do not know if I would have made it and kept my sanity if it had not been for you and Walter. I cannot remember the name of our landlady when we shared the off-campus apartment, but I do remember the name of her son, Tunis. I still think that is such a strange name. Wonder if he still has it, or has changed it to Jack or Bob? I remember my many trips when I would sneak downstairs and turn up the thermostat because it was so cold. It would not be long until she would come out and turn it down again. I was surprised she never caught me doing that.

Remember the day when I was taking the garbage out to the can? I was in the middle of the yard and was loaded down with garbage. You were on the upstairs porch and said in your most godly ministerial voice, "Bob Davis." I immediately dropped the garbage, which scattered, then dropped to my knees, and said, "Yes Lord." You fell down and rolled across the floor with laughter. We did have some good laughs together. That was instrumental in keeping me going. We still manage to get a few good laughs in as we talk.

I still have the letter you wrote to me upon my retirement in

1989. *You said such nice things, and it came at a time when my grief over the loss of work and my then present uncertainty over my tomorrows were heavy upon me. I have been able to adjust somewhat to those feelings, but like all grief, I think it is settled, then some small thing will happen to resurface it. It must be dealt with again. I have read your letter many times and find it comforting and reassuring.*

Thanks for your friendship and for your supportive love that I have felt through the years. It's friends like you who make life meaningful and, in its darkest days, bearable. We really must get together very soon.

A LETTER *to* CARLTON

As happens often with the passing of years, friends who were once close tend to move away, either geographically or by lack of continued familiarity. Most of my father's close friends mentioned in "A Letter to Jackie" remained either in Mississippi or in the area of Memphis, Tennessee. Since he ended up in North Carolina, geographical distance caused them to lose the closeness they shared in their high school days and throughout college.

There was one very special friendship that developed during the 1958–1959 school year at Southern Baptist Seminary in Louisville, Kentucky. Among those about whom my father would often speak were Walter Moore, Jack Causey, Ken Duke, Ed Bailey, Graham Hales, and Carlton Huestess.

He and Jack both ended up in North Carolina and saw or talked with each other often. However, Carlton remained the closest, partly because of geography, but mostly because he was a highly caring and concerned person—one my father considered to be a friend indeed.

Carlton and his wife settled in Rock Hill, South Carolina, and he worked as a pharmaceutical salesman. My father often introduced him as his friend "the drug dealer," but he was quick to give proper explanation as to the meaning of that title!

Dear Carlton,

I found your card at the door last week when we returned from an outing. Sorry that I missed you, as I have sometimes in the past, but glad to let you know that it was an outing and not another stay in Baptist Hospital as it has been on some of your visits in the past. Hopefully, I will not have any more of those visits in the near future, but I have learned to "swing" with them as they become necessary. Since school is out, Harriet and I are able to get out a bit and journey around some. We do not venture far from home, but I do enjoy being able to get out.

Carlton, I cannot begin to express to you what you have meant to me during the past years, especially in the last two or three. I have such fond memories of our days at seminary and the good times we were able to share together. I am very grateful to you for your continued friendship throughout the years, and for your many visits in more recent ones. I know it was, at times, difficult for you to fit me into your very busy schedule, but you always seemed to have a few minutes for me. I always looked forward to your coming and appreciated the short time you were able to give.

Having to quit work as I did was a very difficult experience for me. I had thought I would be able to work until 62, take early retirement, and enjoy a small antique business until Harriet reached retirement age. Then we could enjoy our antiquing together. Ah, but "the best laid plans of mice and men ..." When medical retirement came, I was filled with mixed emotions. A part of me felt some relief because the weakness and nausea had taken a lot of the joy out of my working. So many days it seemed almost impossible to gather the energy to bathe, dress, and drive the twelve miles to work. Being exhausted when I finally arrived there, usually late, I would have to spend the first hour or so on the couch in my office, awaiting renewed energy. If I had not had an understanding supervisor and supportive staff and volunteers, I could not have held on as long as I did.

Another part of me wanted to hold on as long as I could. After all, I was a "people person," and I hated to leave my daily exposure to and involvement with community. As I left community, I knew it would be an adjustment. Several friends were good to call, come by, even to bring lunch in those early days, but that did not last too long. The feelings of isolation quickly set in. It seems that is the time you began to drop by for your regular visits. Several of those times, I found myself at my lowest ebb of isolation, loneliness, and disillusionment with humanity. When I was convinced that the world had forgotten me, that no one cared, and that I was no longer a part of community, you always seemed to appear at my door. How good it was to see you and to be reminded that there was still a caring community out there and that I was not forgotten! You may have experienced some of those feelings when you had your bout with cancer some years ago, so perhaps you can understand my feelings and my deep appreciation to you for your continued friendship, care, and concern. I will always remember you with love and fondness for your support and kindness to me and hope that in some way, some day, I will be able to repay some of it to you.

A LETTER *to the* GLEANERS

My parents moved to Kings Mountain in 1987 and joined the First Baptist Church. About a year later, my mother was asked to be the teacher for the Gleaners Sunday School class. She agreed on the condition that both she and my father could be co-teachers.

They began teaching the class, which was filled with ladies from the age of sixty-six through seventy-two. Over time, some of them came down with the "Jack Benny" syndrome—when he hit thirty-nine, he stayed there, and some of the ladies hit seventy-two and stayed there, so that they wouldn't have to leave my parents' class.

Each summer, rumor would get out that "they" would make the ladies move up to the next class, or "they" were going to split the class since it was so large. The rumors always proved to be false alarms, but they did cause a great deal of stress. My father would try to calm the ladies' fears by reassuring them that "they" could not force them to do anything—after all, wasn't that the Baptist way?

Those ladies became dear to my parents and part of our "family" in the truest sense of the word, continually supporting Mom and Dad with their friendship and love. From the first Sunday my parents walked into the class, they felt the warmth and sincerity of their acceptance. This kindness not only never waned, but it continued to grow. It was a relationship my father cherished and for which he was eternally grateful.

Dear Gleaners,

Little did I know in 1988 when we became teachers for the Gleaners Sunday School class that we would experience the love and caring we found. I had been both pastor and staff member in seven different church-related situations and felt a closeness in two of these. Even so, I am amazed and thrilled at the feeling of acceptance and love I feel as we have grown in our relationship. This is as it should be, and the world would be a better place if all in the church had the same degree of acceptance and caring you have expressed toward us—and toward others as they have become part of the Gleaners Class.

As I have observed a number of churches through the years, it has been my experience that there is a large percentage that do not cater too well to outsiders coming into their fold.

This has always been strange to me, and I know that it is in total opposition to which Christ meant for the church to be. Your spirit of love and acceptance are a refreshing thing in the midst of so many churches that do not seem to have caught the true meaning of churchmanship.

I did not know when we became your teachers that we would have to walk the path of the final stages of kidney failure, dialysis, and transplantation, or that we would walk the path of Harriet's breast cancer. I guess it is a good thing that we do not know what lies around the corners of life, for we might be tempted not to turn the corner.

I feel sometimes that we have become a burden to you. After all, my nine hospital stays in the past two years, and Harriet's recent stay have caused you much extra work. You have been so good to support us with your visits, phone calls, delicious meals, prayers, cards, gifts, and loving and caring friendship. I seriously doubt that we could have survived with any degree of sanity if we had not had you. We lived in virtual isolation, void of love and support, for the nine years in Shelby. We have commented many times, during the time we have been a part of your class, that we are lucky to be in Kings Mountain, and even more lucky to be a part of the Gleaners.

Thank you for all you have done to minister to us, and for the many expressions of your Christian commitment as you have related to us and to others in the church and the community. You are Christ in attitude and action, and I am proud to be a part of you and to have you as my friend. We love you now and always will.

....

SELFLESSNESS

....

$\mathcal{A}$ LETTER *to* SHIRLEY

As the time came for my father to begin dialysis, the public became aware of his battles with kidney failure. Their reaction was a positive experience for him, as he was greeted with much concern and many good wishes. But there were four people who stood out to him as those who went the "extra" mile on his behalf: Wilene Smith, a friend and one of his main office volunteers; my mother's uncle and aunt, Carl and Werdna Black, from Tennessee; and me. I landed on this list because the four of us offered to give my father one of our kidneys. He found this incredibly moving, and we were all grateful to offer, despite the obstacles we would have faced.

The doctor at Baptist Hospital told my father that he was an excellent candidate for a transplant, a fact that surprised him because he thought he had passed the age for transplantation. As I shared in A Letter to an Unknown Donor, the doctor told him (in July of 1989) to get a beeper because that would be the probable way to make contact with him when a kidney became available. So he got a beeper and settled into his daily routine, which included dialysis and waiting for contact with Baptist Hospital. In the meantime, folks in many of the churches in the Kings Mountain Baptist Association had placed my father's name on their prayer list and were praying for him in general, and for a new kidney in particular.

It was in the context of this prayer vigil that the fifth person to go the "extra" mile surfaced. Her name was Shirley Madden, and she was the secretary of the First Baptist Church of Lowell, North Carolina, where my father served as pastor. At that time, she was Shirley Atchley, and through the passing years she had moved to Shelby, North Carolina, divorced, and remarried.

One day in the fall of 1989, my father received a phone call from Shirley. She said that she and her husband, Courtney, wanted to come and talk with him about something. Before the conversation ended, she told him the nature of the impending visit: while at prayer service the Wednesday night prior to her call, she received—along with everyone in attendance—a card with one name on it. The purpose of the card was to pray for the person whose name was on the card. When she looked at the name, she noticed that it was her old boss from Lowell. As she began to pray, she said it suddenly dawned on her that she needed to do more than just pray for him. As he needed a new kidney, and she had two and needed only one, why not give one to Bob Davis? Needless to say, he was overwhelmed. Although the transfer of her kidney to him did not materialize, he was forever grateful for her loving gesture.

Dear Shirley,

It has been some time since we have been in communication. I trust that all is well with you and yours. Things are going well, but slow for me. With the family back into the swing of school, my days are back as usual. I am currently adjusting to the new fall routine, doing some reflections on the past and writing about those reflections.

It is in relation to these reflections to the past that I am writing to you. I will never forget the day of your phone call when you offered me one of your kidneys, or the day of the follow-up visit with you and Courtney. Others had made such offers, but yours, coming out of the blue and in the context of prayer commitment, made it different somehow. That you should even consider such an offer was, in itself, a miracle.

By this time, I had learned to live with miracles because I had experienced a few along the way. But I had never been offered the ultimate gift from anyone with such conviction before. The gift of life was what you were offering me, and I was deeply touched by it. I did not know if the kidney would be a match, or if the possible transplant would become a reality, but at that moment, it did not matter. What did matter was that you cared enough to make the offer, and knowing you, I knew you did it with sincerity and commitment to an accepted task.

The weeks seemed to drag by as we continued to wait for word from the doctor at Baptist Hospital. They did seem to be awfully slow in getting things started, but I'm sure there is a reason behind that. When the call from the transplant team member came in April, I assumed that it was in relation to your donation of a kidney, since you had been to Baptist the week before. We were to hear any moment from them concerning the possibility of a match between your kidney and my body chemistry. As you know, the call turned out differently than I had assumed, and I was given another kidney. I was glad to get it over with and was glad that you were spared that pain and discomfort of the surgery.

I have had the new kidney for almost eighteen months now, and it seems to be doing really well. Though it is not your kidney, I feel that you were very much a part in my getting it. Thank you for your concern for me and for your offer of one of your kidneys, and your willingness to see it through until the transplant could take place. I will be eternally grateful for your generosity, your friendship, and your love that prompted you to make such a moving offer to me.

I wish that many others who are awaiting transplants could have a friend like you. There are over seventeen thousand persons who are waiting, and the sad reality is that many of them will die before transplant can take place. The last figures I saw were that there are about 3,400 donors who have signed donor cards. Not all of them will become actual donors because the final decision must be made by the closest relative, and some circumstances will prevent the donation of organs and tissue. I wish there were more people who would realize the tremendous benefit to thousands and get involved in the organ donor program. We hear a lot about current recycling programs. There is no greater need in our country today then to recycle our parts when we have finished with them.

I recently became acquainted with a couple who has a ten-month-old baby boy named Mark. Mark is a beautiful child, but he has no kidneys and has been on dialysis since he was three months old. I hurt for him and his folks. I hurt for all of the others who suffer organ failure and for their loved ones who helplessly suffer with them. I realize full well that if it were not for caring folks like yourself and the family of the young man who made it possible for me to get a kidney, my family and I would still be suffering the throes of dialysis and the uncertainty of tomorrow. You are indeed a good friend, and I thank you for your concern that led you to this commitment to me. I will be eternally grateful and thank God daily for you.

My best to you and Courtney. May your life together be filled with much happiness and many years.

REGRET

A LETTER *to* VAN

On May 7, 1990, after three weeks in North Carolina Baptist Hospital, my father was to go home to Kings Mountain, North Carolina. On April 18, he had been the recipient of a kidney transplant. That May morning, at a little after seven, the phone rang in his hospital room. It was my cousin Mike, and the news was not good. My father's brother Van had died.

This was a most difficult time for my father. He had been through three weeks of hospitalization preceded by one year of dialysis and was weak to the point of exhaustion. He had temporarily lost the use of his legs and was confined to a wheelchair. Mississippi never seemed farther away. He knew that he could not go for the funeral, and that made a painful situation more difficult. Uncle Van had been gone slightly over a year when he wrote this letter.

⁓

Dear Van,

It seems strange to see the above two words appear on the paper in my typewriter. I know that you cannot receive this communication, for I am not sure of your address or even the zip code. Do you think General Delivery – Heaven would do it? I suppose that will be acceptable. So many things have transpired in my life since the morning that you went away. I do not know if you were aware of it or not, but that day that you left was the day that I was to come home after the transplant. Since that time, I have had to return for four more stays at Baptist Hospital. Because of my own set of circumstances, I find that a lot of days are spent in the reliving of memories. The meaning of life today is no longer dependent on the hopes for tomorrow as it once was but on the touches with the significant people and events of the past. You are a part of those memories.

Didn't we have a time as children? I have often thought that I would like to be able to provide for my three the same experiences that I had as a child. I guess my earliest recollection of events shared by the both of us was the time you made me angry, and I hit you in the head with the wing of my metal airplane—don't remember what you did to deserve such a response, but it is indicative of my presence of a temper. Of

*course, you could aggravate me, and I did respond as I knew
how. Remember when I shot you in the back with the BB gun
or hit you in the head with the knife or threw the rock grenade
on the day the Japanese surrendered World War II and broke
out your front tooth? You could always hit and run and I could
not catch you; however, I did have a pretty good throwing arm
and a good sense of aim.*

*We always did seem to have our difficulties, and until later
years we did not have the closeness that families should have.
Guess that, in part, was due to the geographical differences
that we experienced. Sometimes it seemed that our only
common bond was the fact that we had the same parents. We
were so different; however, in more recent years, that seemed to
change for the better.*

*Yesterday I spent some time watching an old Tarzan
movie. You remember how we liked to go see them years ago,
don't you? They have come out with some old ones on VCR
cassettes now. Ashley and Ashlie gave me one for Father's Day.
As I watched it, I thought of the time we were playing in the
woods at Independence. Actually, Dad had sent us on our late
afternoon chore of driving the cows home for milking. As usual,
we did all we could to make it a fun trip and prolong the
milking tasks as much as possible. At any rate, I climbed the
huge oak tree at the edge of the open pasture. I was nearly to
the top searching for mistletoe, which I had heard had some
magic power that when held over a girl's head would cause her
to respond with a kiss. I was very much interested in trying this
with Shirley, the love of my life at that time. You were also in*

the tree about halfway up. While I was influenced by thoughts of Shirley, you were apparently influenced with thoughts of the Tarzan movie that we had seen the Saturday before. You began to give out the "Tarzan yodel" as you would swing from limb to limb. After several yodels and swings, I heard a thump, but no yodel. You had missed your mark, fallen, and broken your wrist. We hurried home without the cows. You would not go in the house but made me go in and tell Mom and Dad. Off we went to Batesville to the doctor. No cows were brought home that night, and no milking was done.

Then, there was the Tarzan time that you, Billy, and I went to the movie in Oxford. We sat down in the front row—equipped with popcorn and coke, eagerly watching the Tarzan movie. All of a sudden the herd of elephants began to stampede. They seemed to be coming directly at us. Guess we were all sure that they would get us, for we forgot popcorn and coke and ran in fear and haste to the nearest exit. You and Billy ran out the side exit, but I headed for the front door. As I reached the back of the theater, I realized that the stampede was over. I looked around and did not see any of the elephants. Feeling somewhat safe, I found a seat near the back of the theater and settled in to watch the rest of the movie. I was not aware that you and Billy were locked out the side exit, unable to re-enter. As I was engrossed in the movie, I heard someone call my name. It was the usher. Dad had come to find me because you and Billy, unable to get back in the movie, had gone home without me. We did have some times, didn't we?

I really did appreciate your weekly phone calls and your

visit during the year that I was on dialysis. We were looking
forward to the week that you had said you would come and
visit last June. Little did I know at that time that you would
not be here to make that trip. Your daily phone calls, while I
was in the hospital for the transplant, were both assuring and
comforting, and I miss the present times that we cannot talk. I
really thought that I would be the first to depart but guess it
was not to be. I know that you told us of your illness, but we
had no idea that things were as bad for you as they turned out
to be. I think that was partly due to the distance between us,
and partly due to the fact that you continued to work five days
a week, spend every weekend at the flea market, and
participate in your National Guard responsibilities. I felt that
if you were as sick as you said you were, you would not be able
to keep up that pace. I guess that is based on how I felt while in
kidney failure. I was so sick and weak most of the time that I
found it impossible to go to work or do the fun things.

I will always regret that I was not able to come for the
funeral. Even now, I find some difficulty in realizing that you
are no longer with us. Intellectually, I know it is true but
emotionally, it is a different matter. I think that is because I
was not able to be there and share in that time with the rest of
the family. Mom, Dad, and Rebecca kept me informed on a
daily basis of the events as they took place. They each
reported on the many floral arrangements and the multitude
of friends who came to pay their respects. I wonder, why do
we always wait for death to send the flowers? It would have
been so nice for you if you could have enjoyed your flowers

while you lived! Guess the funerals of life are not for the dead but for the living.

Somehow, because I was not able to come to the funeral, I never did get to say good-bye to you. Not that you would have heard me, but I could have had that opportunity to begin the closure that is so important to the grieving process. So, I am writing to thank you for your concern in our later years and to let you know that though we were not as close as we could have been through the years, I appreciate what we were able to share for the last three years. So, with these thoughts, I will say good-bye to you. I miss you, and even though we never spoke of our love for each other, I do love you and the memories that have surfaced anew and afresh since you have gone on from us. By the way, do they have a flea market in heaven? Hope so, and hope to see you there someday.

INTERNAL CONFLICT

A LETTER *to* AUNT LELA

In my grandfather's family, there were eight children—four daughters and four sons. The daughters were Lela, Lilly, Bess, and Lucille. The sons were Curtis, Lee, Van (my grandfather), and Richard. My father talked of all of them often, and he remembered each of the girls for special reasons.

Aunt Lilly was the "corset" lady. She sold and always

wore a tightly laced Spencer corset. Aunt 'Cile was the sewing lady, and most importantly, my father's college mother while he attended the University of Mississippi at Oxford, where she lived.

Aunt Bess was the one who told stories to my father as a child, and he remembered her cooking, especially her chicken pie. And Aunt Lela was the one who had money, wore tattered sweaters with the elbows worn through, and was religious. Not that the others were void of religion, but Aunt Lela seemed to have an abundance. Because of this, as my father reflected on his life in the ministry, he wrote of his religious pilgrimage to Aunt Lela.

Dear Aunt Lela,

I am sure you will be surprised to hear from me after all these years and the many miles that separate us. I wanted to write to bring you up to date on my religious pilgrimage since I last saw you. I remember your religious devotion and feel that you, of all Dad's people, will be interested in what has happened to me.

I think that the last time I was in your home was when I attended Boys State in Jackson. You and Uncle Carr were so kind to come and get me for supper and to go to the Billy Graham Crusade that night. Then, on the weekend, you came for me, and I spent the weekend in your home. I remember the first meal of the weekend. It began with each person reciting their favorite verse of scripture. We did not do that at our house, and I did not know what to say as my time approached.

I remember the feeling of panic as my turn came near. When my turn came, I timidly mumbled the only verse I could remember: "Jesus wept." That brings a chuckle to me now, but it wasn't amusing then. You were kind enough that you complimented me on my selection and did not laugh at me. That night, in my room, I was determined that I would be ready for the breakfast reciting, so I got the Bible and began searching for a verse. When breakfast came, I could hardly wait to redeem myself. My turn came and I spoke with confidence and enthusiasm. "Righteousness exalteth a nation, but sin is a reproach to any people." To this day, every time I think of a verse of scripture, that one comes to mind.

I don't think I ever told you, but the visits with you to the Billy Graham Crusade were not my first. A year or so before that, I had gone with the youth from our church to the Billy Graham Crusade in Memphis, Tennessee. That was an experience that was to change the course of my life as soon as I would allow it to do so. On that night in Crump Stadium, I felt the presence of God as I had not felt it before, and I learned firsthand the meaning of the phrase—"being born again." Strangely enough, it was with this same experience that I heard God tell me that He wanted me to preach. I was quite willing to accept the forgiveness and the salvation, but the rest of the experience seemed impossible to me. Surely, I had misunderstood that part of the message. Yet, the message kept coming to me. "I want you to go and preach," He kept saying. I had been taught that God was all knowing and all wise. Surely He must be making a mistake here. Me, preach? I felt totally inadequate to do that. I could not speak in public. I did not consider myself intelligent enough for the task. I know that I was not perfect, and I really thought you had to be perfect in order to serve God in that manner. And I, of all people, was not perfection. I have since observed a large number of preachers who display enormous levels of imperfections. So, I guess that I must fit right in with the rest of the saved sinners!

At any rate, after about four years of running away from God and His calling and telling Him all the while that He did not know what He was doing, I said, "Okay, I'll do it, but You'll have to take charge and tell me what to do each step of the way." Guess that was what He wanted to hear all the while because it worked. Isn't it wonderful that He is so patient with us?

That next fall I went to Mississippi College, which turned into a most delightful experience! After graduation the next spring and a refreshing summer at home, I left for Louisville, Kentucky, to attend the Southern Baptist Theological Seminary to further prepare for the task before me. That first year proved to be a disaster for me, and again, I began to think that either God did not know what He was doing or that I was interpreting the message wrongly. You see, my year at Mississippi College had been such a spiritual growth time that I assumed that the seminary would bring me an even closer step to heaven.

It was during this first year that I became keenly aware that not all Christians act like Christians. Competition was so fierce that some students would not offer a helping hand to others for fear of having someone else get the better grade. Some professors seemed cold and uncaring. That was a year of unrest and upheaval among the faculty and ended with thirteen of them being fired as a result of what seemed to me to be a power struggle between them and the president. It about proved to be too much for the green, naïve kid from Mississippi who thought he was going to get a glimpse of heaven.

Somehow, I survived and graduated in May of 1957 with a Master of Religious Education degree. I later went back and got the Master of Divinity degree. I pastored four churches and worked as the Minister of Education in one other before taking a position as Church and Community Ministries Director under the appointment with the Home Mission Board. I held this position until I was forced to take disability retirement due to kidney failure.

That, in a too long nutshell, is what I wanted you to know. The road has not always been easy, but it has definitely had its rewards. I would so love to be able to return to active ministry, but the kidney failure has caused a condition called peripheral neuropathy, and mine is so severe that I have lost a great deal of use of my hands and lower legs. This is very frustrating and causes much grief and anger within me. Some of my friends speak in compliments of my positive attitude and courage as I attempt to deal with life as it has come to me. They do not see the inner struggle to try constantly to overcome the feeling of worthlessness and depression that is present with every waking hour. Because of the loss in function of hands and feet, a lot of things have to be done for me. The thought came to me last week that I have become an inconvenience. I am struggling *with that thought as I write to you and trying to get on top of the resulting depression rather than having it on top of me. I wonder, were you having feelings of being an inconvenience that day some thirty-seven years ago when you took your Bible, went into the bathroom, read your scripture, perhaps said your prayers, and tied the cord of the Venetian blind around your neck and took your life? I wonder.*

DEVOTION

noun | [dih-voh-shun]

a feeling of strong love or loyalty; the quality of being devoted; the use of time, money, energy, etc., for a particular purpose

Devoting oneself to a cause or another person—or even a deity—is not an act to be taken lightly. It is to submit yourself fully, entrusting your soul and your being to the recipient. This is what my father did for the people and experiences in his life.

Since I was a child, the word devotion has run through my life like a golden thread. Its religious implications certainly held sway over my parents' lives for many years. This reality was not surprising, as being devoted is an essential part of the religious, and in particular the ministerial experience. It is an almost blind devotion that allows one to endeavor upon the acts needed as a servant to a higher purpose—lost weekends, missed experiences, long days, service to others, the list goes on. But it's also crucial to note that devotion solely for devotion's sake serves little purpose.

To fully understand and appreciate the act of devotion, one has to live a purposeful life. At its core, devotion is an act of love. Love is something we all search for and feel, but devotion is love with a higher calling. That higher calling need not be within a spiritual confine—yours can certainly be different from mine or your spouse's or your parents'. But devotion does involve a complex set of emotions and commitment, whether to another person, a faith, or a cause. You give a piece of yourself. You sacrifice. You compromise. It is selfless and it is true.

Love is not about liking, loving, and caring,
but appreciation, understanding, and devotion.
—M.F. Moonzajer

Devotion, perhaps even more than love, gives our lives meaning and soul. There is a song by The Avett Brothers called "The Once and Future Carpenter." In that song is a line that says, "If I live the life I'm given, I won't be scared to die." If one reads between the lines, devotion lies at the core of that sentiment. It causes one to think, Have I determined my dreams? Chased my dreams? Fulfilled my dreams? Devoted myself to my dreams?

Answering your calling, using your gifts to their full potential, those are the things to which one should focus his or her devotion. There is a lot of talk in today's culture about finding one's "purpose," and that is certainly a good start. But discovering one's purpose and actually fulfilling one's purpose are two different things.

My father always encouraged us to "do what we are supposed to do," which meant living a live of giving, of renewing, and of sustainability—of essentially living the golden rule.

While my father was fairly liberal in his social approaches to life, he certainly possessed and communicated a clear understanding to his boys what they should and should not do. I'm not implying that I always took that advice (there is, after all, a reason they refer to us as Preacher's Kids), but I did know that if I strayed, there would be consequences.

As I said in a previous chapter, I found great pride in my father's leadership in the church, both in the community and in the pulpit. However, I also learned that his modicum of celebrity could be used against me.

One Sunday morning when I was around nine years old, I was having a difficult time focusing about midway through the sermon. As a good PK, I was in the front pew of the church with a clear line of sight to Dad. As his delivery of the story of Noah, or Job, or Adam and Eve, or whatever he was imparting to the congregation began to rise in intensity, so did my inability to sit quietly. It was then that my father said in his beautiful, baritone Southern drawl, "... And God said to ... Ashley!" Then, with a slight pause and a sly grin, all was quiet and my father continued with the lesson. From that point I sat quietly, having learned a lesson from a man of devotion—not only to God and his congregation but to his child—a man who was committed to raising a son who would one day hopefully show that same devotion and care to the raising of his own children.

Without devotion, action and knowledge are cold and dry,
and may even become shackles.
—Unknown

Love is a beautiful feeling and motivates numerous benevolent actions, but devotion brings true meaning to those actions. Some find that meaning through religious devotion, while others find it in their family, community, or friendships. But no matter where it is found, that devotion to others was a fundamental part of who my father was—and of the letters that follow. It is illustrated in the young love that emerges for so many in college, then meanders through life with ups and downs, eventually sustained by the very devotion with which it was created. It is seen in the love of a caring mother who nurtured a young, humble boy into a proficient man of God. It is witnessed in a father, who having lived through the hardships of the rural south in the 1920s, displayed love in a far more stoic, yet no less sincere manner. It is displayed in the letters my father wrote to his boys—my brothers and me—he loved so dearly. Finally, it is shown in the comfort and solace my father found in a Creator he was introduced to in a public setting, and who found His way into the most private and vulnerable aspects of his life.

Always there comes an hour when one is weary of one's work and devotion to duty, and all one craves for is a loved face, the warmth and wonder of a loving heart.
—Albert Camus

 LETTER *to* WILLIE

In 1942, my father was in the second grade at Independence School near Batesville, Mississippi. His family lived nine miles from town, so because my grandfather was principal of the school and my grandmother taught fifth and sixth grades, they lived next door to the school in the "teacherage," a four-room house with a "path." (For those unfamiliar with this term, it refers to the outhouse, as there was no indoor plumbing in those days.)

Rural Mississippi had none of the finer things in life in my father's younger years. They relied on kerosene lamps in lieu of electricity, and they had a wooden icebox on the back porch instead of a refrigerator. The "path" wasn't even theirs; it was located behind the schoolhouse some distance away.

As progress began to reach their community, they acquired electricity and bought a refrigerator for the kitchen. Next, the large iron cooking stove was replaced with a shiny electric Kelvinator. Sometime later, the "path" was substituted by a small room added to the side of the house that contained a small sink, a large tub, and a "gizmo" upon which one could sit and not have to worry about spiders and other creepy things getting you. Progress was deemed to be a wonderful thing, and my father recounted that there were many exciting innovations and events taking place during that time.

One of the progressive happenings was the realization that the species of mankind was divided into basic groupings—male and female, or in my father's understanding, boys and girls. He was not sure as a seven-year-old what exactly the difference was, but somehow the girls of the species seemed to look better than the boys. It was in the context of this realization that he felt the first pangs of infatuation. Her name was Mary Alice, and all the boys thought she was the cutest in the class. His best friend, Billy, thought she liked him, but my father was certain that he was the favored one. At least some days it seemed that way.

The third grade brought a new room, a new teacher, and a new love in my father's life. Her name was Emma Helen. This may cause a chuckle should any of my father's third grade friends read this, as this was his first infatuation with an older woman. You see, Emma Helen was his teacher. Of course, he did not call her Emma Helen, but rather, Miss Emma Helen. My father claims she was a real beauty and that he worshipped her. He would often reflect on his feelings of rejection on the day a tall, handsome man in a white uniform appeared at the classroom door. He and his classmates quickly learned that the man was Miss Emma Helen's boyfriend, home on leave from the Navy, and that they were to be married. The third grade boy who was to become my father was crushed.

In the years to come, my father had crushes on Mary, Betty, Mary Agnes, Ann, Nancy Ball, JoAnn, Jocelyn, and Carolyn. But none were as powerful as the one he had on Willie. Once she arrived on the scene, it ended his search for the perfect love. For those wondering about this (as my mother's name is Harriet), you will naturally assume that he didn't marry Willie. But keep reading ...

During my father's second year at the seminary, his job was cashier in the school cafeteria. This had many benefits, among which was an opportunity to observe the single female species as soon as they hit campus. It was in this capacity that he first noticed the girl he called Willie.

Wilma Harriet Black was from Saluda, South Carolina, and went by Harriet. (She was one of many people in my father's life who disliked her first name, so I hope she will forgive me for telling you.) It was many months before she would tell my father her first name. Then she threatened his life should he, in a weak moment, let it out. Through the years, he began to call her Willamena, which gradually and affectionately came to be Willie.

Dear Willie,

It has been a quiet Sunday afternoon for me since you and the boys are in Saluda for the birthday festivities. Suppose at this late hour you are on your way home. I have the Vince Gill CD on and he is currently singing "Look at Us," which is, as you know, one of my favorites. "Look at us after all these years together!" Who could I think of except you?

Here we are, thirty-three going on thirty-four. I remember your dad's trying to get us to hold off on the wedding until he could build a new house. Thank goodness you did not fall for that. Wasn't it some twelve or thirteen years later that they finally completed the new house? I am glad we did not waste those years. I guess since kidney failure and transplant, the days

we have are more precious than they ever were. I know that I
live on borrowed time, and that makes every day with you more
special than the days that have gone by. Yesterday is gone,
tomorrow is yet to come, but today is ours and I am keenly
aware that all these years together serve as the foundation for
what we have today.

"Look at you, still pretty as a picture." Vince continues to
sing. I suspect that he must have had you in mind as he wrote
these words, even though you are not known to him. It does
seem to me that you get better looking as the years go by. Here I
am with worn-out parts and there you are, going strong and
looking better every year. Who would have thought that the
young lady from the house with the fallen-down picket fence in
Saluda would grow to the modern-day beauty you have
become!

I remember the first time I saw you. It was in the cafeteria
at seminary, and I was at the cash register when you came
down the serving line. All of us singles who were second-year
students were anxious to see the "new crop" of young ladies
who had come to study that fall. I had the advantage over the
others, being the cashier and everyone having to come past me.
As I took everyone's money, I had the opportunity to size people
up and get acquainted. And there you were, pretty as a picture,
and fresh out of the academic fields of Limestone College.
Things did not go so well for us at first. Being your first
semester, you thought you were to put all of your time into
study, but being my third semester, I had realized there had to
be more to seminary life than study. I am afraid at times I took

that attitude too far, but we made it to May of 1960 and graduation, didn't we?

"Look at us, still leaning on each other." After thirty-three years, we are still leaning on each other. As you have often commented, "When it comes down to the survivals in life, all we have is each other." We have had to lean heavily during the past five years especially. I sometimes feel that I do most of the leaning, and you have to do most of the supporting of the leaner. Kidney failure, dialysis, transplantation, and my many stays in the hospital have taken their toll on our energies, but you seem to be able to cope with it all. I'll bet when you said "For better or worse" on July 23, 1960, you had no idea what was in store for us. I guess it's good that the future is clouded for us. If we knew what it held, we might run and hide.

Then, there was the day that the big "C" came to us. I'll never forget that phone call from Dr. Plonk. "Carcinoma," he said. You were so strong. I think the three years of tending to me and my kidney failure prepared you for that day, for you had developed a sense of independence and inner strength during my three years of leaning on you.

As I considered the presence of cancer, I had an overwhelming feeling. For the first time in our thirty-one years, there was the possibility that you could go first and I would be the one left here to survive alone. That had never crossed my mind. I was the one with health problems and had always assumed that my life would be shorter because of them. Now uncertainty for our tomorrows loomed in the future from a different perspective. How grateful I am for mammograms, Dr.

Plonk, Baptist Hospital, Dr. Muss, and yes, even for the chemotherapy with all its bad side effects. Two years have come and gone since that day, and you continue to get those good reports that say, "Cancer free!"

The years have come and gone too quickly. Sometimes I think it would be great if we could pick out the best ones and live them over again. No changes, just enjoy them again as we did the first time around. It would be a difficult task, and I would probably end up picking the same thirty-three again. So, here we are, three sons, seven churches, and one association later. Life has certainly been good to us, and now we have Lisa and Ashlie (the two daughters we never had) and Kristi, our four-year-old bundle of joy. I get so amused at her when she calls me "her little Papaw." Her sense of size is interesting. Guess sometime down the future road, we will have that third daughter as Benji nears marriage age, whatever that is.

So, we look forward to the "Golden Years" and retirement. Of course, retirement will be nothing for me since I had to take medical disability in '89, but it seems to be something to which you look forward. Don't know how many years we will have to continue to "lean on each other," but I am determined to take each on as they come and enjoy them to the fullest.

Thanks for the thirty-three, and all of the joy and sense of satisfaction and accomplishment you have brought me. Most of all, thanks for loving me in spite of myself and standing by me during all these years, especially since 1988. I know it has not been easy. We have seen so many who have separated as a result of kidney failure and all of the stress that this sickness puts on a marriage. It seems to have made ours stronger, rather than weaker, and for that I am thankful. I love you for being you and for giving me all that you have given. Thank you for "still believing in forever." Who knows, perhaps "in a hundred years from now, they'll all look back and wonder how we made it all work out." But we did, didn't we?

A LETTER to MOM

My grandmother, or Nana as I called her, was a Barbee (not the doll) before her marriage to my grandfather. My father was never one to dwell on ancestry, but he had a cousin back in Mississippi who did considerable research on the Barbees of the world, and he supplied us with some interesting facts concerning the family tree.

The family name was originally Barby, and the first mention of the name can be found in records kept by William the Conqueror, who in 1065 listed three Barbys as minor tenants. We don't know what the word "minor" means in this case, but it was apparently our beginning point. We may have even come over on the Mayflower! That makes our family a pretty old bunch.

In the early 1800s, Elijah Barbee of South Carolina married Monica Poe of North Carolina, and they settled in Alabama. In 1803 they are recorded in county records as having sold some land in Alabama. The couple had three sons: Jesse, James, and Thomas, the last of whom was born in

1831. He married Susan Morgan and settled in Coahoma County, Mississippi, where he died in 1865 near the end of the Civil War. Thomas was my great-great-grandfather.

An interesting story about Thomas ...

He was shot in the back, reportedly by General Forest of the Confederate Army. My grandpa, when he told the story, said that Thomas was a deserter, and that as he ran, General Forest shot him as such. The Barbees, however, told it a bit differently. Their version is that General Forest's men came to Thomas's plantation and took all of his mules, promising to leave him one so that the land could be tilled for the next year's crop. However, the soldiers did not leave a single one, so Thomas went to retrieve his one promised mule. Apparently, there was some trouble, and as he took the mule, General Forest shot him in the back and killed him. We don't know which account is accurate; both may be wrong for all I know, but it's an intriguing piece of our ancestry nonetheless.

Thomas and Susan had three children: John, Amelia, and Ophelia. John was my great-grandfather (he seemed to like married life since there are five recorded marriages for him and several offspring); his final marriage was to my great-grandmother, Virginia (Jennie) Gordon Hall, and they produced namesakes Amelia and Ophelia (my grandmother). In all, there was a total of fourteen children.

My grandmother was only six when her father John died. Six years later, as I mentioned in A Letter to Jackie Hunt, her mother closed the large home in the delta of Mississippi and eventually settled in Blue Mountain, Mississippi, a college town where her girls could be educated. She ran a boarding house next to the college and both my grandmother and her sister graduated from Blue Mountain.

In 1931, Ophelia married Van Davis, and they had four children: Lavanda Lee, Robert Gray (my father), Steven (stillborn), and Rebecca Ann. By this time, never liking the name Ophelia, Nana unofficially added Ann as her middle name, and that was the name she chose to use. It would seem that my father had two loves of his life who did not care for their first names. One reason for the addition of Ann as a name, besides the fact that she did not like Ophelia, was that she had a friend in school whose name was Ophelia Butts. As a writer, I must admit here that you can't make something like that up ... and as you can imagine, she was the butt of quite a few jokes!

Life was not easy for Van and Ann. During the Great Depression, school teachers in Mississippi were not paid very much, and sometimes they were given an IOU instead of a paycheck. According to Peanut (that's what I called my grandfather, which was based on the fact that he was a peanut farmer for a portion of his career), some of those IOUs were paid and some were not. Then, when my father was six weeks old, my grandparents went to a movie in town, and when they returned home that night, the house had burned to the ground. Nothing was saved except for a straight chair from my great-grandmother Jennie's boarding house in Blue Mountain. Someone had seen the flames and came running to help, only to find that there was nothing that could be done. Peanut grabbed the chair from the porch and saved it. My father kept that chair at the desk in his den as a reminder of hard times, and of his parents who would not give up, determined to start again.

In 1950, my grandparents stopped teaching and moved back to the Mississippi Delta to Lula. They were married for a devoted sixty-one years.

Dear Mom,

How we did enjoy your recent visit with us! The week passed too quickly, and you were on your way back to Arkansas. We will look forward to your return in October for another few days together. Isn't the space age wonderful in that it makes Arkansas only a couple of hours from North Carolina? I'll bet those of the pioneer days would look at today's generation with amazement and envy.

It is hard to realize that Dad, Van Jr., and Meme have gone, and we are left to endure. I surely thought that I would be the first to make the homeward journey, but here I am enjoying each day and waiting to claim my mansion. Some days get a little rough, and I have to fight the feelings of despair and depression. As I look back over the years, I realize that you and Dad have given me the examples of endurance and the will to continue in spite of the odds. Even in Dad's departure, I saw you with all of your strength go through his funeral, leave your home of seventeen years, and begin again. Such courage has to be admired! Not many of today's generation are made that way.

I'm grateful to God who has allowed me to have you as my

mom for these fifty-nine years. You are very special and have given me so much during my lifetime. I have such warm and wonderful memories of childhood. I remember those hot summer days before electricity came to rural Mississippi. Each night I would go to sleep with your fanning me to help me to cool off. Then came winter and its coldness. Our heat was a fireplace where one could warm only one side at a time. Each night you would take the brick from the fire, wrap it in a towel, and place it at the foot of the bed so that the sheets would not be cold. I know you must have gotten tired of all that fanning and heating of bricks to warm the bed, but you never quit.

I remember the horse that Mr. Jack Hawkins had in his pasture that bordered our yard. The cows in the pasture did not bother me. I guess that is because we had cows, and I was used to them. The horse was a different matter. I was sure he was out to eat me. Many a night I would dream that the horse was sticking his head through the window at the bed and was determined to have me as his next meal. You were always there to wake me from my nightmare and assure me that all was well. It was a long time later that I was convinced the horse would not eat me but was more interested in the grass that grew in the yard outside my window. At any rate, other than the horse nightmares, life as a child was secure. I am thankful to you for making it so.

You and Dad taught me so many of the values of life that I still hold to be true today. I remember, in particular, one thing you taught me that has been a most valuable lesson throughout my lifetime. On our usual Saturday trips to town, we quite

often would see Annie, a wretch of a person. She reminds me a
lot of those I have seen in person or in newspapers and
magazines of today's world. Today they are often referred to as
"bag ladies." I guess there was no name for them then. She was
a fright to me, and I always got close to you when we would see
her. She was an addict, as I remember. Many called her "paregoric
Annie." She would beg money in order to go to the drug store
and get paregoric, which she apparently consumed by the
bottle. Each time you would see her, you would say, "There, but
for the grace of God, go I," and it would help me to view people
with a sense of compassion rather than a sense of judgment.
You, by your example, helped me to have a compassionate view
of life, and I still have it today, though the years and
circumstances have taken their toll on my supply of patience.

I am grateful for the years of training you gave me in the
matters of God's love. Those years as a child at the Presbyterian
Church in the Independence community are as vivid to me
today as they were then. My most cherished memories are of
summers and Vacation Bible School. Often we would meet
outside under the large oak trees and have our lesson for the
day. I remember the Biblical figures we would make of
clothespins, crêpe paper, and glue. I still have the plaque made
from macaroni letters: "Man shall not live by bread alone, but
by every word that proceeds out of the mouth of God." It is a
wonder the bugs have not eaten it in all these years. On and
on, the warm memories flow through my head. I have attempted
to give my three boys such a part of their memory bank, but I
know theirs could not be as good as mine in spite of my attempts.

One memory stands out from my days at Lula-Rich High School. It is not such a warm memory, but one that I have anyway. You were always such a good cook and your reputation as a baker of cakes was known far and wide. That year, at The Halloween Carnival, you were asked to bake one of your famous caramel cakes and to place something in it so that folks could pay a quarter and guess. The one who guessed it would win the cake.

I'll never forget that night! You had told me the secret ingredient to the cake—a half pecan placed in the middle between the two layers. Everyone looked with watering mouths at your cake; it was the talk of the adults at the carnival. Then, Miss Millie Sanders, the first grade teacher, approached me in the hallway. "Did [I] know what was in the cake?" she asked. Yes, I said. After all, she was not only an adult, she was also a teacher. You had taught me to be honest and respect my adults, especially my teachers. Those values proved to be my downfall.

She pressed me for an answer, and after several attempts on her part, and her following me down the hall, I told her of your secret pecan half in the middle of the cake. When the winner of the cake was announced, everyone was delighted that it was Miss Millie—everyone except me. I was too consumed with guilt to be excited. Somehow my values of respect for adults, especially teachers, and to be honest at all times was lacking in something. I had obeyed my teachings, but felt terrible that I had told. As I look back on it now, I think that someone had not taught Miss Millie to respect me, or she would not have pestered me so. That was one of those unforgettable happenings in life that has stayed with me until this day. I do not see caramel or pecan halves without thinking of that night and Miss Millie.

We are enjoying the things you have given us from the house when you left Mississippi to move to Arkansas, but they are just things. The real gifts have been your guidance, love, and direction throughout life. You have given me many things for which I am most grateful. Most of all, you gave me a Mother's love that was untiring and unfailing. No matter the circumstances, you have always been there to give your support and encouragement. As I reached adulthood, you were able to cut the "apron strings" and let me flounder on my own two feet, yet remain close enough to pick up the pieces should I fall. I have done the same with my three and realize that it is not always the easy pattern for the parent, but it is the most beneficial for the child. Thank you for each and every cherished memory and all of the good times we shared as a family. I will be eternally grateful for God's giving me a mom such as you.

I hope this finds you going well today. You have been through so much in the last year, but you seem to have such a determination to overcome. I'm sure there are not many who could have gone through the loss of a spouse of sixty-one years —and the loss of a home—in one week's time and handled it as beautifully as you did. You are an inspiration to all of us. We admire your stamina and courage. Life gives us some hard knocks sometimes. Hopefully, I will be able to handle mine as you have handled yours. Guess I'd best close. Let us hear as you have time. I love you, Mom.

$\mathcal{A}$ LETTER *to* DAD

My father had many fond memories of visiting his grandparents on his father's side of the family tree, Richard Henry Lee and Lena Benton Davis. Their rambling house with many rooms included a pump organ, which was a forbidden instrument for the grandchildren (not that they didn't try to sneak in to play it), and the upstairs was a series of unfinished rooms except for one. My father was always fearful of going up those narrow stairs because it was spooky to him, and he was sure some evil monster was lurking in the dark corners of those unfinished rooms.

When my grandparents (Ophelia and Van) had their first child, Aunt Lillie and Aunt Lela both told my grandmother that she should name the newborn son after his father, which was Lavanda Lee (you can see why he went by Van). I have no idea where Peanut was during this time, but his son was named on the basis of his two sisters' recommendation.

Despite being called "Bo" most of his life, Lavanda Lee disliked his name until the day of his departure from this earth on May 7, 1990. My father always said that Aunt Lillie must have laced her "Spencer" too tight that day and circulation to her brain was affected. It wasn't until several years later that Grandma realized she had been hoodwinked by Lillie and Lela. She did learn her lesson, though. When it was time for my aunt to be born, Aunt Lillie told Nana that if it was a girl, she should be named Lillie Lela. But my grandparents in their wisdom named her Rebecca Ann, much to my beloved aunt's applause. I'm sure she had a deep sense of appreciation that Nana had learned not to listen to Aunt Lillie when it came to naming the children.

My grandfather, like a number of men in his day, and perhaps today also, was not a man who expressed a great deal of affection. For many years, my father wondered if he was loved, because his father never spoke of love that he could remember. For a long time, he was sure that his dad loved his brother, Lavanda Lee, but not him. As he looked back over the years, he remarked that he could see the many expressions of unspoken love, but because the words were not there, he doubted. I always found this interesting as I grew older because Peanut was so loving and kind to his grandchildren. Sitting on his knee and lighting his pipe was one of the joys I so looked forward to on our long drives from North Carolina to Mississippi to see Nana and Peanut.

My father once shared an incident that happened on a visit to his grandparents' house. It was during the Christmas gathering, the one time that all the children and grandchildren were together. Junior Carr, Aunt Lela's son, was always called on by his mother to give a recitation as the adults sat at the table and ate Christmas dinner. The rest of the grandchildren thought this was amusing, since they were not required to attend and were therefore able to take their chicken and go eat on the front porch. (All the grandchildren had to have the dark meat except for Billy and Mary Bess, Aunt Cile's children, who always got to have the white meat.)

About this same time, Lavanda Lee had been tested at school and proven to have a very high IQ. That fact, plus Junior's recitation, was the talk of the dinner table. Later in the day, the grandchildren were all in the yard playing while Aunt Lillie and Aunt Lela sat on the front porch watching. My father was close to them and overheard part of their conversation. One of them said, "Aren't Junior and Bo so smart? I think Junior will make a lawyer, and Bo will be a doctor." The other agreed and added, "Yes, I think you're right. I wonder what will happen to poor little Bobby (my father) and Billy?" That stuck in my father's mind for many years— that notion that poor little Bobby probably would not amount to much.

Later that evening, Aunt Lillie's boarder, Bernice, wanted to know who belonged to each of Aunt Lillie's brothers and sisters. When she came to my father, he told her that he was Van's son. Her response was, "Well, they must have gotten you at a blanket party. You don't look like anybody." The others thought that was funny, but my father was crushed. Not only was he "poor little Bobby," but he did not look like anyone in the family. Then to top it off, his father never told him he loved him. Years later, he was able to look back on it all and have a hearty chuckle—by then he knew that he was indeed somebody, that he had found his calling, and that his dad did love him.

A few years before my grandfather died, he and my father talked on the phone. For several years during my father's time of increasing kidney failure and dialysis, they were not able to make the trip to Mississippi. Nana and Peanut came to North Carolina as they could, but most of their visits were by phone. One day as they were finishing their conversation, my father said, "Dad, I love you." Like my grandfather, my father wasn't accustomed to offering verbal affection (though he always did with my brothers and me—it was important to him that we hear it as well as see it). After a few moments of silence, my grandfather said, "Well, we think a lot of you, too." My father knew (and even chuckled) as he put down the phone that that was as close as he would probably get to hearing those three important words.

Dear Dad,

So many days have come and gone since Bob called me on the morning of November 20 to give me the news about your departure. It was so strange. I had just finished talking with Rebecca about our concerns over your impending chemotherapy and the ill effect that it would have on you and Mom. We both felt so helpless because we knew what was in store for you, and we knew that Mom would not be able to handle the situation alone. We also knew that it was impossible for us to be there to help out the whole time.

I had often wondered how it would feel to lose a parent. Harriet and I had both often commented about how blessed we were to be our age and still have all four parents living. About five minutes after Rebecca and I had finished our conversation and concluded that we could do nothing about the situation except to sit and worry, Bob called. The message was short. "Dr. Lloyd just called. Van died this morning."

My mind went in several directions. How could that be? I had just talked with Rebecca, and she said nothing about your dying. Surely something was wrong here, but I soon realized

*that it was reality. My dad had died, and Mom was there
alone. I have felt very far from home on several occasions, but
this time I felt farther away than I had ever felt before. At the
same time, I found an amazing sense of relief. Now, my dad
would not have to experience the awful pains of chemotherapy
—the awful pain of going through the doors of death with lung
cancer. Mom would not have to see you suffer as Uncle Lee
had suffered. I know that had been much on your thoughts
since he had died with lung cancer. So many emotions, but the
emotion of rejoicing over your departing with as little ease and
pain as you did was the overriding emotion for me. I felt that
God had been so good to me to give you to me for all these
years, and then to take you quickly was surely a blessed relief to
me and to the rest of the family.*

*Your departure did accomplish one thing that I had
considered to be impossible. Harriet got on a plane! You know
that she had said for years that she would never get on an
airplane. When I called Gray to tell him of the news, he
contacted Lisa, and she began to make the arrangements. She
was so good to help us. I had thought that Gray and I would
fly, and Ashley, Benji, and Harriet would drive down. Well,
much to my surprise, Harriet volunteered to fly. So, on
Saturday morning, Harriet, Gray, Benji, and I boarded the
plane for Birmingham. Davis met us there and took us on to
Starkville. On Sunday, Lisa, Kristi, and Ashley flew down, and
Gray and Benji went to get them. Ashley and Benji flew back
on Tuesday, and Gray stayed with us until after Thanksgiving.
Mom and Rebecca had decided that they wanted me to have*

the Cadillac, so we brought it back with us and are enjoying it.

The funeral service was so nice. Dr. Lloyd and Brother Andrews did a superb job. I had asked that it be short because I knew it would be better on Mom, and I had been told that Dr. Lloyd, like so many of the clergy, could be long-winded.

The highlight of the service came at the end. I sat next to Mom, Harriet next to me, and Kristi next to her. As the service was concluded, the funeral home folks were rolling you out the side door; Kristi stood close to Mamaw Harriet, put her little hand up to wave to you, and said, "Bye bye, Peanut." That about did it for Harriet and me. We had both tried to be brave for Mom's sake.

The six grandsons served as pallbearers and looked so nice dressed in their dark suits. Mom said you would be so proud of them. Speaking of Mom, you would be so proud of her. She has had her rough moments but has handled them beautifully. She realized soon after your death that it would be impossible for her to stay by herself, so the transition was easy for her. After Thanksgiving, she went to Arkansas to live with Rebecca. Shortly thereafter, we succeeded in cleaning out the house, each of us getting some things. The house sold in March, and the final exodus for each of us was in April.

Starkville is still there, but home is not. That has been more difficult for me because for the first time in almost sixty years, there is no home to go to visit. I have to take comfort in the saying, "Home is where the heart is," so a part of home is here in North Carolina, part in Arkansas, and part there where you are. One day it will all come together, and we will dwell where

*you dwell. Hopefully, we who remain here will find departure
as easy as you did, but we'll have to wait and see about that.*

I have spent so many hours since your death reliving the
memories of days gone by. This is partly due to my own
limitations brought on by kidney failure and the neuropathy,
and partly because of the vacuum created by your departure.
Often my memory trips take me all the way back to
Independence and to the good days of childhood. You have left
me, all of us, with so many memories. These revisits to the past
serve as a great source of comfort.

I remember those late summer evenings when we sat on the
porch and played in the yard. You would put me on your
shoulders and run around the house, much to my delight. After
several trips around the house, you would stop running. I'm
sure you were exhausted at that point. I would say, "Just one
more time, Daddy," and off you would go, time and time again,
never seeming to be tired—always willing to heed those magic
words, "Just one more time, Daddy."

I remember the summers when you worked for the ASCS
office, leaving early in the morning and returning late in the
afternoon. You always had something for me. I remember
sitting on the front steps each evening waiting for you. Each
day, you would bring the little brown paper sack in which
Mom had packed your lunch that day. There was always a
piece of a sandwich, a cookie, or a piece of candy for me. I
looked forward to my very own picnic on the front steps. Years
later, as I worked those hot summer days for the ASCS, I ate all
of my lunch and thought of you as you put some aside each day

for the little boy who sat on the steps and waited—an act of love, much like the "Just one more time, Daddy" events in my life. These events continued throughout your time here. I am grateful for these and for all you did for me.

I have hoped to be able to leave my three boys with memories equal to those you left me. I am thankful that when adulthood came to me you were able to stand back and let go and let me be me. Mistakes were made in my standing, but you were always there to help and support and take me one more time "around the house."

My branch of the tree seems to be going well. Harriet has been free of her cancer for two years now, and my borrowed kidney has worked well for over three years. Gray, Lisa, and Kristi are well. Kristi calls me her little Papaw. Don't know where she got that little part. Ashley and Ashlie married in December and are doing well. They recently moved into their new home. Benji is starting his second year in college and working part-time at a local video store here in Kings Mountain. He is such a help to me. We will surely miss him when he goes to UNCC after this year.

Got to go for sure this time. Guess you are aware "up" there that Meme died. That has hit Mom hard, but she does well with her losses.

Dad, we miss you but are grateful that your journey here is over for you and that you now dwell in that place "where there is no sorrow, no more pain, and no more death." I love you. Thanks for being my dad, and for being there when I needed you, and for still being there in my many wonderful and cherished memories. I look forward to the day when we shall meet again and feel confident that we will.

 LETTER *to* GOD

There were numerous things that impressed my father the many times he watched *The Color Purple*. One of them was Celie's short, open conversations that began "Dear God."

He felt highly fortunate to have been born to Van and Ann Davis. They gave him many blessings, the greatest of which was an early awareness of the presence of the love of God. My father could not write of significant people, places, and events, and not write his feelings of devotion to Him.

Dear God,

I cannot tell you the first time I became aware of your existence. It was a very long time ago and I was a mere toddler. Memories of those early years are not with me but I do know that you were there. I was being introduced to you through my parents, Christian friends, and your church congregation.

I want to thank you for placing my care with my parents. I am so grateful that they were yours and trained me in your direction. I know that the ultimate decision of an individual in relationship with You has to come from that individual, but I am a firm believer in Your Word that says, "Train up a child in the way ... and when he is old he will not depart from it." My parents were trainers, and I am grateful to them for their dedication and faithfulness to you.

My earliest years of training were at a small Presbyterian church in a community known as Independence, Mississippi. I have such fond memories of those years. Independence was a community centered on an elementary school and a country store. Life was simple and seemed uncomplicated compared to life today. My folks were Baptist, but the Presbyterian Church was closer to us. Those were the years of World War II when gas and tires were rationed, so we went to the closer church.

The great excitement of the summer was Vacation Bible School. A lot of the time we met outside under the shade tree. There, I was introduced to people of the Bible like Abraham, Moses, David, Samson, Jesus, Paul, and so many others. I was told you were a God of judgment, wrath, and vengeance, and that if I was not a good boy, you would get me. I am sorry to tell you this, but I do not remember being told that you were a God of supreme love, complete forgiveness, and total acceptance of me as a person. It was years later before I became aware of these qualities.

My training in Your way was spent with a great deal of things that I should not do. These were the "do-not's" of religion. Some examples were: do not dance, do not smoke, do not drink, do not play cards, do not fish on Sunday, etc. There did not seem to be anything that one could do. The problem was that no one ever told me what I should do. It all began to *fall into perspective years later when I found the "Thou shall love the Lord your God" verse of scripture. I have often commented to Harriet that you must be tired of being blamed for everything and of hearing the "do-not's" of your people here. You are truly a God of patience.*

I joined the church and was baptized when I was nine, but I guess you know that. I made what I understood was a profession of faith at that time. As I look back on it now, I'm not sure that I was doing anything except following in my brother's footsteps. I did a lot of that in those days. It was a beginning, though, and it was to grow into a greater fullness some years later.

When I was sixteen, I met You on a very personal and powerful basis and have continued that personal relationship since that night at Crump Stadium in Memphis, Tennessee. You became more than the name "God," and You became more than "somebody up there." You became a positive factor, and I wondered even more why I had been taught the negatives about You. I still run into those negative "do-not's" and am quick to tell the positive "do's" when I encounter the negative.

I am grateful for salvation, my continual forgiveness from You, and Your continual presence of direction and support. Your love is so overwhelming to me. I know it is not anything I deserve, yet because I was created in Your image and have a part of You in me, I have become special. Thank you for that.

Thank you also for the leadership and direction You have given me throughout all of these years. Thank you for Harriet and the three boys You have given to us. These four, and now Gray's Lisa and Kristi, and Ashley's Ashlie are my pride and joy. Thank you for the multitude of friends who have been willing to love and accept me in spite of my sometimes unloveliness. Thank you for the security of my tomorrows. I have traveled through some rough waters in these few years. Thank you for Your presence through all of that. I know that this is an incomplete list because there is so much that You have done for me. I could not begin to list them all.

There is one request that I would make to you. Do you suppose that You would stop the neuropathy in my left hand? I know You could, but would You? I would so love to have its present usage. I would like to have it restored, but I can get by if it just doesn't get any worse. I would also like to be able to return to active ministry. I still feel that deep sense of calling to serve You. It's frustrating not to be able to do what You have called me to do. I know You understand that it is an impossible task with my present disabling circumstances, but it sure would be nice to be able to pastor Your people once again.

Guess I'd best close. I wonder, do You get tired of reading? Perhaps I should not have rattled on for so long.

....

PATERNAL AFFECTION

....

$\mathcal{L}$ ETTERS *to* THE BOYS

‹ ⚬ ›

The marriage of Robert G. Davis of Lula, Mississippi, to Harriet Black of Saluda, South Carolina, in 1960 resulted in the birth of three children. Born in 1963 was Robert G. Davis, Jr. My father was opposed to giving him this name for fear he would be called Bobby or Junior; he wanted to name him Steven Ashley. But after three days of debate and the insistence of the nurses that he had to have a name, my mother instructed the nurses in my father's momentary absence to name him Robert Gray Davis, Jr. As if my father had a choice, he reluctantly agreed with the understanding that the baby would be called Gray. As that was my father's middle name, the middle name of one of my uncles, and the maiden name of my father's grandmother, they would be carrying on a family tradition.

Their second child was born in 1968 when my parents were back in the seminary. It was January and they had twelve inches of snow on the ground. After arriving at the hospital around nine-thirty on a Sunday night, the doctor came out at ten forty-five and told my father that he could go home because it would be morning before anything happened. Five minutes later, the doctor came back and said, "Don't leave. The baby will be here in a few minutes." And at seven minutes after eleven, the second offspring for Bob and Harriet came into the world.

Thinking this would be a girl, they had picked two names: Sally Ann, which my mother favored, and Allison Edwards, which my father favored. Well, so much for that. It was another boy—my father could at last have his Steven Ashley. Alas, my mother intervened once again and wanted to name him for her father and my grandfather—William and Van respectively. That seemed okay to my father, but he couldn't help but wonder, how many children were they to have before he got a Steven Ashley?

Believing that two children were enough, he suggested they compromise and name the new bundle of joy William Van-Ashley. My mother agreed. Though he lost the name Steven, he had his Ashley at last. (Guess you can tell that he was influenced by *Gone with the Wind*, which he had seen ten times, at least.)

In January of 1973, while living in Covington, Virginia, my mother fell sick with the flu that had made its rounds in the church and community. While most people recovered from their bouts, hers continued for several weeks and included periodic visits to the doctor. Finally, after weeks of nausea, weakness, and continued lack of energy, my father said to her, "Do you suppose you're pregnant?" It seemed a foolish question, as two doctors had told her that because of a medical condition, it would be impossible for her to become pregnant again. Talk about "famous last words"!

On October 3, 1973, their third son was born, and gone forever were the names Sally Ann and Allison Edwards. They had not considered a boy's name; after all, they had used them all except Steven, and my father did not like that name without the Ashley. So after much discussion, they decided on the name Benjamin Trotter Davis, and that they would call him Benji. (Trotter was for my mother's Aunt Fannie, and Benjamin was a biblical name that meant "beloved son," which proved to be true.) Actually, all three of his sons were beloved, but how could they have three Benjamins in the same house? Who would come when he called?

This reminds me of a story my father told about when they lived at Curtis Station. It was cold and my father and Uncle Bo had the responsibility of getting up each morning, on an alternating basis, to build a fire in the stove in the living room. This was their only source of heat in the house except when their mother was cooking at the far end of the house.

That morning, he heard his father say, "Bobby, get up and build the fire." It was unusually cold that morning and he did not want to move from under the covers. He laid very still, not wanting his father to know he was awake. After a few minutes, my grandfather called again, and still my father did not respond. He heard his name called several more times but remained silent through all of it. He guessed his father must have grown weary of calling him because the next time he called, he said, "Bo, get up and build a fire." Before he realized the significance of what he was doing, my father nudged Bo, who lay in the bed next to him, and said, "Bo, Dad said to get up and build a fire." Boy, did he catch it from the other room! He got up, posthaste, and soon there was a fire in the stove. If he had named all of us Benjamin, who would have built the fire?

A LETTER to GRAY

‹ ═══◈═══ ›

Dear Gray,

Little did I know when you were on your way twenty-eight years ago that I would be writing you this letter. I remember the excitement I felt when we learned that we were going to have a baby. We were living in Shelbyville, Kentucky, at the time, and your mom had gone to a doctor in Louisville. He told us the good news, and my immediate urge was to tell everyone. Since she was only six weeks pregnant, your mom thought it best not to tell it yet. That was a hard secret to keep.

I decided after a few days to go and buy maternity clothes. I went to Louisville and bought some, thinking that your mother would feel obligated to wear them. Then, everyone would know and I could begin to talk about your arrival. It did not work, for she did not need them at that time and thought it foolish of me to want her to wear maternity clothes when she was not "showing," as they said in those days. I was quite proud of my accomplishment and wanted everyone to know.

In proper time, you arrived and were the most exciting thing we had experienced since the marriage. Our nights of good sleep had ended, though. You were a thumb-sucker rather than taking a pacifier. Several times at night one of us would have to get up and find your thumb for you. As you would look for it, it would turn inward into your hand and somehow you could not figure out how to turn it outward and catch hold of it. *After a few nights of our assistance, you finally figured it out and we all were able to get a good night's sleep again.*

When you were six weeks old, we returned to the seminary for me to work on another degree. That was a long summer because I had taken you and your mother to Saluda to stay with her parents until I could move, get a job, and get started in school. The both of you returned in late August and we settled into a routine in Seminary Village.

In March of 1964 we moved to Indiana where I got a church. Boy, was that a learning experience! We were there for three years, then back to the seminary. While we were in Indiana, you learned many words, among which was "spook." For a while, "spook" was pronounced "pook" and you used it for anything unusual or unattractive.

I will never forget the time you escaped from the workers in the church nursery. It was at the end of the service one morning and I had gone to the entrance door to greet people as they left. You were about eighteen months old and here you came, scrambling through the crowd. I caught you before you could get out the door and held you in my arms as I continued to greet people. Up walked one of the deacon's wives. She was a dear, sweet lady, but I was sure that she must have taken "ugly" pills for most of her life. She was short, heavy, wrinkled, and had several teeth missing. As I held you and greeted her, she began to talk with you and held your hand. Very quickly you got loose from her and with both your hands you took my face, turned it toward your face, and with much enthusiasm and wide eyes, you said, "Pook, Daddy, Pook!" I could have died there on the spot. She said, "Oh! Ain't he cute! What did he say?" That was the one time the pastor lied to the deacon's wife, for I said, "Oh, I don't know. He jabbers like that all the time." Boy, was that a close call!

Christmas of 1966 proved to be an interesting time. By that time, your mother had secured a teaching job in Vernon, Indiana, some miles from where we lived. That meant we would no longer have to struggle on fifty dollars a week. Though we were not rich, we could afford more than before. We had a friend who owned an antique shop in Vernon and about once a week, we would stop by his shop for a visit. He had a small oak desk just at the entrance to the shop. This is the desk that you now have in Kristi's room. You really liked that desk and each time we went, you stopped there and colored in coloring books he had gotten for you.

One day I told your mother that we should get the desk for your "Santa Claus" that Christmas. So, we began to pay a little along and got it paid off in late November. We were so pleased and began to talk of "Santa's" bringing it to you. You seemed pleased, and we were too, for the big gift at Christmas had been secured and payment was completed. However, our satisfaction was short-lived because you decided in December that you would not ask Santa to bring the desk. I was crushed. What were we to do? The desk was ours and we had no more money for big items. We decided Santa would have to bring the desk and that we would have to live with the consequences.

I will never forget the happenings of Christmas morning. We got up and Santa had neatly placed several small items on and around the little oak desk. I thought it all looked so great. About that time you walked into the room, looked at your goodies for a moment, then went to the fireplace, leaned over into the chimney opening, looked up and said, "You dumb ole Santa. I told you I did not want this desk!" I was crushed, your mother cried, and I spent the rest of the day thankful that you thought Santa had done it and not I. By the way, hang onto that desk. It was a salesman's sample and it is quite valuable in the antique market today.

When we moved to Virginia, you began to have real skill in the area of athletics, especially basketball and football. You brought home several trophies, winning first place in Pass, Punt, and Kick competition and second place in the state competition in the Dribble and Shoot competition. This was a pattern you continued to develop throughout your high school and college days. We have spent many an hour going up and down the roads to see you perform. How proud we were of your many accomplishments! I never could figure out where you got all that talent and athletic ability. You surely did not get it from your dear old dad. Must have been a hidden gene back there somewhere.

So, now you are grown, educated, and on the road to success. I do not know where that road will lead you, but don't forget to take the time to enjoy Lisa and Kristi and other children, should there be any. Believe me, the years do pass quickly and before you know it, Kristi will be grown and gone. I know you have said that you will not allow her to date until she is forty, but that time will come.

I hope things continue to go well for you and that all your dreams will become reality. Thanks for all the memories you have given to us and for all the joy you have brought. I am proud of you and love you.

A LETTER *to* BENJI

Dear Benji,

It is a cool, rainy day here. It has all the appearance of a fall day and with school having recently begun again, I guess it is time for fall to appear. For the past eighteen years as fall approached, I was always reminded of the day you came to live with us. You were our surprise package, for after the birth of Ashley, your mom was told that she could not become pregnant again.

For the first six weeks of your growing, we were told you were the flu. We were surprised when we found out that this flu was to last for nine months and would not end until October 3rd. It was a rough nine months for your mom, for she was sick —morning and evening—the whole time. It had not been that way with the other two, and all the good ladies of the church assured us that this was a girl. I held out for the name Allison Edwards, and your mom held out for Sally Ann. This all proved to no avail, for when you appeared the doctor said, "It's a boy!" I have wondered over these eighteen years who would have won the naming battle. I did not have a good track record

*in that field, for your mother had won that battle both times we
had gone to war. We soon decided on the name Benjamin
Trotter Davis and you became our Benji. Sometime later, we
began to notice the Benji movies being advertised and were
pleased that they had decided to name a movie after you.*

*You were the best baby. The day we brought you home,
your mother fed you at midnight and you slept until noon the
next day. We kept going in to look at you to be sure you were
breathing, and you were, so we did not wake you. Your mom
wanted to breastfeed you. She had wanted to do that with Ashley,
but the milk truck never came by our house, and after three
days of waiting, the nurses insisted that he be put on formula.*

*There was a good "Baptist" nurse there with your mom,
and when she told her of the problem with breastfeeding
Ashley, she had a solution. She told her to have me get a
certain brand of beer and for your mom to drink a can in the
morning and a can at night. Then, there would be plenty of
milk for you. Now, how would it look for the pastor of the
leading Baptist church in the community to be seen pushing a
buggy filled with beer up to the checkout counter? That would
have raised eyebrows, wouldn't it? Also, how would your
grandmother react? She had been a very ardent member and
supporter of the WCTU back in South Carolina and your
own beloved mother had won many WCTU contests in her
younger years. Here I was at a crossroads of life. "To beer, or
not to beer," that was the question. So, taking charge, I began
the weekly trips to a town twenty-five miles away and across
the state line of West Virginia to keep your mom supplied with*

her beer, and you supplied with "beer" milk. I always felt a bit of guilt with each trip, but it surely did work. Perhaps this is the reason you slept so well and were such a good baby.

After you had been home for three days, one of the good ladies of the church came calling. I was standing in the hallway holding you as she came into the house. As we talked, you gave the appearance of a smile when I spoke to her. She marveled at that and said, "Bob, that baby smiled at you. He knows your voice already." I swelled with pride, even though I suspected it was more of a reaction to gas than to my voice. You see, she did not know about my trips to West Virginia.

We left Virginia in May of the following year and became Tar-Heels. It was shortly after that that Mary Goodlett came to be part of our lives. Your mom began teaching, and Mary came to the house each day except Friday to keep you. There soon developed a bond of love between the two of you, and I knew that I could trust your very life to Mary. She was a quiet lady and of the old school of morals and values of life. She took care of you until we moved to Shelby four years later. We tried to get her to go with us and make her home with us, but we could not talk her into it. She had become a vital part of our family by this time and it was hard to leave her behind.

One of the delightful things about our move to Shelby, and my new work, was that I would, at last, have the opportunity to sit with the family during the worship service. Before this, I was always in the pulpit, you were in the nursery, and Mom, Gray, and Ashley were in the pew. We were a family divided. Now, we could be together.

I remember one Sunday in particular as we sat together. I was on the end of the center aisle of the pew and you were sitting next to me. After the service had begun, you became sleepy and put your head in my lap. I thought you had gone to sleep, for you were so quiet and still. They had planned an ordination service that day for a newly elected deacon. You had never seen one of those. When they called for the ordained people to come forward for the "laying on of the hands," I did not attempt to go because I knew it would wake you. As the procedure started, everything got very quiet. You suddenly became aware of the quietness and sat up to see what was going on. You moved in front of me and peeped around the corner of the pew. It must have seemed a strange sight for a four-year-old. You watched for a few moments as one by one the ordained men walked past the kneeling candidate, leaned over with their hands on his head, and whispered in his ear. After a few moments of watching, you turned to me and said in a whisper so loud that it must have been heard four rows in front and in back of us, "Dad, why are they smelling that man's hair?" I laughed until the pew shook, and so did some of the others.

When you were eight, you had your accident on the bicycle. That was a terrible experience, but you endured it like a trooper. There was the long wait in the emergency room, the three hours of surgery, and the three weeks of traction in the hospital—three weeks of hanging by your elbow. I do not know how you managed that except that you had an innate stamina and strength to endure it all.

You have always done us proud. The move to Kings Mountain and your involvement on the swim team has brought you much recognition and many awards. Getting the award for the most outstanding male swimmer this year was great! We are proud for you and of you. And now, you will soon be eighteen and have recently joined the National Guard. You are the only one of the three boys to have expressed an interest in such. But, then, you were the one who expressed an interest in the Boy Scouts. You seemed to be the joiner in the group. Gray did join the Scouts, but after two meetings decided that it was not for him.

Remember the time you went to camp and we came up on Thursday night for parents' night? You wanted to come home with us but I insisted you stay. I knew that if you came home early, you would have to deal with failure in your first camping experience. If you stayed the other two nights, you could come home with a feeling of success. I wanted that for you. It was a tough decision, for I wanted you home with me.

When you became fourteen, my kidney failure began to escalate and the neuropathy worsened. It became necessary for you to help in my getting dressed. There were so many things that I needed you to do for me. I hated that, for it did not seem fair for you to have to be burdened with doing things for me. Things did not get better, and then came the year of dialysis. You were a trooper through it all. I am very grateful that the unexpected third child came to live with us back there in Virginia. You have brought much joy and satisfaction to me in my aging years.

One of my goals developed in the midst of kidney failure, and its implication is to be able to live long enough to see you grown and established in life. With this new kidney, I feel like I will be able to accomplish that and will watch with a great sense of pride and satisfaction as you are able to get that done. I love you and wish only the very best for you. You have a wealth of friends and have a sense of maturity far beyond your eighteen years. Best of luck always, and take my love with you wherever you go.

A LETTER *to* ASHLEY

Dear Ashley,

It was a cold, snowy day in January of 1968. Your mom and I had returned to seminary that fall, along with Gray who was five at the time. We had learned in May that you were on your way. The four of us had spent the summer in Newport News, Virginia, where I worked as a summer worker in one of the churches. The doctor had told us to look for your arrival on or about December 5, so we started looking in early December. My, you were a stubborn one!

Your mother went to the doctor on a weekly basis, and each week he told her that the next time he saw her would be in the hospital. You were six weeks late. What happened?! I was interim pastor at a church in Indiana and each time I went, I was aware of your impending arrival. Those were long days for all of us.

When you did finally decide to make an appearance, you did it with haste. You were something else. You were almost ten pounds and were very plump and alert, with no redness and eyes open. Your mom still says you were the prettiest baby she has ever seen. I thought you looked like a little Buddha doll and soon began to refer to you as my Buddha baby. Later, this was changed to Budd. I called you that until Hazel McCommas, the nursery worker at Ceredo, West Virginia, told me that if I continued, you would never get rid of the nickname. So, I quit, and you became my Ashley, which is as it should have been all along.

When you were almost four years old, we moved to Covington, Virginia. Gray and I went there and because of your mom's work, you and she stayed in Ceredo and came to Covington on weekends. This lasted for five weeks.

Do you remember the time of your swing accident? You and Sherri Napier were playing on her swing set, swinging as high as you could, then seeing how far you could jump. The last time you tried it, you had your middle finger in the link of the chain rather than around it. You jumped and proceeded to hang by your finger, separating the last joint of the finger. Your mom called me two days later and told me they were getting ready to take you to surgery. A pin would have to be put into your finger to save the use of it. I called one of the church members and made arrangements for Gray's care and started my four-hour journey to be with you and your mom. As I walked into your room, I heard one nurse say to another one, "That must be the father. I sure am glad he's here." But I learned that I had missed all of the excitement. Your surgery was over and you were sleeping.

Before surgery, as they came to give you the "happy" shot, you managed to escape and hide behind the medicine cabinet. Everyone was in a state of panic and your mom was president of that state. Security was called, elevators were checked, nurses scrambled, but you were safe behind the medicine cabinet. Your mom was furious because she had offered to hold you while they gave the shot, but they had ordered her out of the room. Some nurses, I have learned, think they know it all and resent the parent or family for their suggestions. Guess you taught them a lesson. Do you suppose this experience has any bearing on your present fear of needles?

That summer we went to Foreign Missions Week at Ridgecrest. I had fallen and injured my leg and was in a cast. You were in a cast up to your elbow. Everyone felt sorry for us and wanted to know if we were in an automobile accident. I did not tell them that I was accident prone and that you had inherited that quality from me.

We have had some good years. You have always brought me much joy, and I have loved you for that, as well as for the many other fine qualities you have. Your sensitivity toward others and your sense of caring for your fellow man have always impressed me.

I remember once when you were in the eighth grade and I went to see one of your teachers to see how things were going. Of course, she gave glowing reports of you and that pleased me. She asked what I did, and when I told her about my work with the Juvenile Court Camping Ministry and your going with me to the sessions, she said, "Well, that explains a lot. I've noticed that Ashley relates really well with the kids who are always in trouble, many of whom are impoverished. They really like Ashley, and now I know why he is that way. You have taught him to be a caring person." To hear that expressed by her made me feel more proud than if she had said you were an A student.

I will never forget your phone call to me while I was in Baptist Hospital getting started on dialysis. You were in Charlotte at the time but had not attended school that semester. You said, "Dad, can I come home? I feel that I can be a help to you and Mom, and I would like to come back home for a while." As if you had to ask! You were such a help to me during that year of dialysis. I hate that you missed out on a year of school and graduating with your friends, but I do not know how we would have made it without your being here to help. Thanks for that and for all the thoughtful things you have done and continue to do for us.

I hope all your tomorrows will bring you all the happiness you deserve. Life should prove to be a joy for you, for you have been the source of joy to so many. Your mom and I have often commented that you will have a hard time deciding on whom to include in your wedding for you seem to have a multitude of friends.

Always know that I love you and appreciate you for the child you were and for the man you have become. Enjoy life each day, for in reality, today is all we have. I have become keenly aware of that because of dialysis and transplantation. Take care.

$\mathcal{A}$ CALL *to* ACTION

It is my hope that the letters you've just read have touched you, made you smile, or caused you to reflect on your own life. But I also hope they have inspired you to consider your own letter-writing journey—no doubt there is at least one person who would be overjoyed to receive your written gratitude for their role in your life, for asking forgiveness or owning regret, or for something they did for you that changed you for the better.

I recently had lunch with a dear friend of mine named Sara, a former colleague from my days in the corporate world. She had gone through a rough twelve months—her mother passed away, her father was diagnosed with dementia, her brother-in-law was diagnosed with cancer, and her 45-year-old husband recently underwent open-heart surgery. To say her spirit had been tested would be an understatement, but through it all she remained strong and positive.

After chatting for a few minutes, I asked her a simple question: "When was the last time you wrote someone a letter?" There was a short pause. "Writing notes and cards was a staple from childhood," she said, "but with everything going on lately, it's been a long time since I've done it."

A few days after our conversation, she sent me a note to let me know she had written a letter to her brother-in-law who had just been readmitted to the hospital. The sense of joy and compassion she felt by sharing her thoughts with him was overwhelming. She closed her note to me with the following: "Thank you for asking me that question. Time is of the essence." Soon after this exchange, her brother-in-law passed away, making her words that much more profound.

People often have the best intentions after reading a book like this—but what's important is the action you take. It's easy to make that mental list of those you'd like to reach out to, but it's another to actually take the time to do it. So what I ask of you is this:

Make that list. Write down the names of people who have influenced you, moved you, made you a better person, or deserve your apology. Then choose one—someone you know can reach by mail—and carve out some space in your day to write that heartfelt letter. The joy you will feel in doing so, and the delight the recipient will receive is immeasurable. Once you have written one letter, you will likely feel encouraged to write another ... and another ... until the movement I hope to foster takes hold throughout the nation—and the world.

Yes, soundbites may work in some arenas, but for heartfelt expression, we need to reclaim handwritten communication with fully spelled-out words and a signature at the end that isn't automatically generated by our email settings. We should not wait another day to tell someone how much they've meant to us in one capacity or another. Let's be inspired by my ailing father's efforts to offer appreciation, to express regret, to make amends, to open his heart ...

Let's start a movement to create a Life Through Letters.

QUESTIONS FOR DISCUSSION

1. In Letter to Stone Man, Robert Davis learns a valuable lesson about empathy. What are your thoughts on his decision as a boy? On what happened to him as a man? Have you had a similar experience?

2. In Letter to Brother Andrews and Letter to Ray, the virtues of being a good pastor are discussed. Do you agree with Mr. Davis's opinion? What are your expectations of the role of the clergy?

3. What was your reaction to Claude in Letter to Claude? Would you have the capacity to sit with someone in his condition? Why or why not?

4. Have you ever expressed gratitude to inanimate objects as in Letter to a Pill? If so, to what and why?

5. In a world where people are often judged prematurely when replacing another in an important leadership role, Letter to Church Friends offers both sides of assuming that role. What did you think of the congregation? Of how Mr. Davis handled the transition?

6. In Letter to Helen, in what ways is altruism shown in its highest form?

7. How is the hospital, in Letter to a Hospital, portrayed in human form?

8. What are your thoughts about organ donation and confidentiality in Letter to an Unknown Donor? Do you believe a recipient has the right to meet the donor's family, or at the very least be able to give the family a letter of appreciation through a third party? Is it fair for a donor family to refuse communication with the recipient?

9. In Letter to Rebecca, what is your perspective on Mr. Davis's specific memories with his sister? Do you have similar standout memories with your sibling(s)? Do you know if they share the same memories or remember them differently?

10. Have you ever had a relative like in Letter to Aunt Fannie? What warm memories do you possess of this person?

11. In Letter to Jackie Hunt, Mr. Davis highlights one particular friend from high school and her immense impact on him. Was there someone in your high school or college days who changed the course of your life without knowing it?

12. Why do you think Mr. Davis found it important to write to "Jack" in Letter to Richard Wayne and to Carlton in Letter to Carlton? What do the letters say about male friendships?

13. Mr. Davis was sometimes at odds with how fellowship was or was not embraced in the churches where he worked. How, in Letter to the Gleaners, is fellowship inherent in their faith? Why do you think some congregations are not this way?

14. Selflessness is personified in Letter to Shirley. Do you think you could ever consider donating a kidney? If so, under what circumstances?

15. In Letter to Van, specific sibling memories come to the surface. How are they different from those in Letter to Rebecca? Have you experienced similar detachment or regret in a sibling relationship? Why do you think it was present? Have things changed with time, like for Mr. Davis and his brother?

16. Letter to Aunt Lela presents a shocking ending. Why do you think Mr. Davis chose to write her this particular letter in light of her decision to take her own life?

17. In Letter to Willie, Mr. Davis waxes reminiscent on his marriage. Do you think this type of reflection often highlights the best parts of a relationship? Do you believe that the longer the marriage, the more good is remembered? Why or why not?

18. As in other letters to relatives, Letter to Mom highlights specific memories. Why do you think these stood out for Mr. Davis?

19. Fathers sometimes have difficulty conveying affection to their sons, as in Letter to Dad, but not to their grandchildren. Why do you think this is? How did Mr. Davis's lack of affection from his father influence the man he became?

20. If God knows everything about us, why do you think there's value in writing Him a letter? Do you believe it has the power to strengthen the bond between you?

21. In Letters to the Boys, Mr. Davis writes separately to each of his sons. What common threads do you see in the letters?

22. How has this book inspired you to write letters? Who immediately comes to mind as a person to whom you wish to reach out? How do you imagine the letter could impact that person's life? Your life?

JOIN THE COMMUNITY

There are several ways you can become part of the Life Through Letters community.

1. Write a meaningful letter to someone who has touched your life.

    Then:

2. Submit your letter, along with the story of its impact, at info@alifethroughletters.com to be featured on our website and social media.

3. Tweet your featured story on Twitter using @AshDavisLetters, #alifethroughletters, and a link to www.alifethroughletters.com.

4. Snap a photo of your letter and post it to Instragram with the tag @AshDavisLetters and #alifethrough-letters.

5. Follow us on Facebook at A Life Through Letters.

We look forward to having you join us!

www.alifethroughletters.com

ACKNOWLEDGMENTS

This book would not have been possible without the early direction and mentorship of Lolly Daskal. Thank you for all your help. Kendall Hinesley kept me on track in organizing the details that formulated the book's foundation. Thanks also to Stacey Aaronson for your heartfelt guidance and input in taking this project from a book idea to a living, breathing tribute to my father.

Profound thanks to my father, Robert G. Davis, who was my inspiration in life and the inspiration for this book. Thanks to my mother Harriet Davis who taught me so much, including the importance of writing. Thanks to my brothers Gray and Benji for your support of this project and your friendship through the years. My aunt, Rebecca "Baba" Thomasson, served as inspiration and support for many years to my father. Your assistance in his early effort at his collection of letters led to the creation of this book. Your love and support of this project and for me is immensely appreciated.

An immense thanks to my beautiful wife and best friend Juhayna. You have been part of the journey for this book since the beginning. From the original three-ring binder that contained my father's letters to the leather-bound adaptation you created of his writings, you have shown compassion and love for the project and for me. I will be eternally grateful for both. I love you.

To my sons Laith and Kais. I hope this book serves both as a reflection on your grandfather and his life, as well as a guidepost for you as you navigate the life that is to come. I love you dearly.

ABOUT THE AUTHOR

ASHLEY DAVIS was born the middle son to a preacher and a teacher, and spent his first years of life in the fields of Indiana, the coal mines of West Virginia, and the mountains of Virginia, finally settling in North Carolina by age five. After graduating from the University of North Carolina at Charlotte with a degree in English, he spent his career in media and advertising. His corporate experience was focused intently on communication and building relationships, vital disciplines passed down to him from his parents. Devoted to community and charity, Ashley volunteers extensively and finds great joy in his role as a husband and father. He lives in North Carolina with his wife and two children.

A Life Through Letters is his first book and a tender tribute to his beloved father.

THE MAN WHO INSPIRED
A LIFE THROUGH LETTERS

ROBERT G. DAVIS was born in Mississippi and held degrees from Mississippi College and the Southern Baptist Theological Seminary. He served as full-time minister of education or pastor in five churches in Kentucky, Indiana, West Virginia, Virginia, and North Carolina, from 1960 to 1978. Appointed a career missionary by the Southern Baptist Home Mission Board in 1978, he served as director of church and community ministries for the Kings Mountain Baptist Association in Shelby, North Carolina, until forced into retirement by a medical disability in 1989. He received numerous ministerial and community service awards.

Mr. Davis passed away in 1997, leaving behind his wife Harriet and three grown children.

70496651R00112

Made in the USA
Columbia, SC
10 May 2017